# THE WEALTH PLAYBOOK

# THE WEALTH PLAYBOOK

## YOUR ULTIMATE GUIDE TO FINANCIAL SECURITY

### ANDREW BAXTER

# ACKNOWLEDGEMENTS

I would like to thank all the team that made this book possible, taking it from the whiteboard through to what you see today.

I would like to recognise Kewyn Appadoo for his unshakeable belief in the project and our journey, Mitch Olarenshaw for his constant motivation and Ben Avery for his attention to detail. Also my parents, for instilling in me the values I continue to hold dear to this day, which I trust I have passed on to you, as a reader of this book. More than anyone though, my wife Emma. Each day, your support, patience, understanding and sacrifice make everything possible.

Finally, I would like to acknowledge you, the reader, for trusting me with your time and reading this book. I hope it has provided you with a game plan, deeper knowledge and the motivation to kick the goals you desire. Now go and make it happen!

First published in 2024 by Andrew Baxter

A catalogue entry for this book is available from the National Library of Australia.

All inquiries should be made to the author.

Printed in Australia

ISBN: 978-1-923007-35-2

Project management and text design by Publish Central
Cover design by Pipeline Design

**Disclaimer**
All materials in this publication are of the nature of general comment only and do not constitute professional advice or individual advice in any way. These materials are not intended to provide specific guidance for particular circumstances and should not be relied upon as the basis for any decision, either to take action or not take action, on any matter which is covered. We strongly recommend readers obtain professional advice, where appropriate, before making any decisions. To the maximum extent permitted by law, both the author and publisher disclaim all responsibility and liability to any person, arising directly or indirectly from any person taking or not taking action, based on the information in this publication.

# CONTENTS

# INTRODUCTION

If you have picked up this book, it's likely because you're looking for more out of life. That could mean more money, more time for fun, more choices, more security – or all of the above.

Let me tell you – you're not alone. We all have dreams, goals and aspirations. And, for me, they emerged in my earliest days growing up as an only child in the working-class town of Swindon in south-west England.

## MY STORY

If you've heard of Swindon, it's probably through Ricky Gervais' mockumentary sitcom *The Office*, where he jokes that if an atomic bomb hit the town, it would only cause 'about 15 quids worth of damage'. While that might be a little harsh, it is fair to say my childhood was far from glamorous.

Don't get me wrong – my parents ensured we were never broke. My dad spent long days at a car factory, while my mum worked tirelessly as a cleaner. They had an unwavering work ethic that meant we always had food on the table and the main things we needed – we were happy!

Even with their constant hustle and steadfast commitment to saving, they just couldn't seem to get ahead. At the time, I was naive – we were the same as everyone else living on our street – and that just seemed like our lot in life.

I then remember reading through the *National Geographic* magazines my dad brought home from the factory and getting hooked on the ads for Rolex watches. How could anyone afford to wear tens of thousands of pounds on their wrist, when most folks I knew were struggling to pay the mortgage?

That kind of curiosity ultimately took me on a journey a boy from Swindon could never have even dreamed of. Today, I'm a multi-millionaire, living on our family farm in Australia's picturesque Byron Bay. The best part? The only person I have to answer to is my lovely wife, Emma!

## Starting with a simple goal

My journey to success began when I was 14 years old. Back then, I had a simple goal: to earn money – step one in the process!

I had an after school part-time job at a local bakery, which paid a whopping one pound an hour! That may not seem like much nowadays but, at the time, I was thrilled. I was not only making money, but also genuinely enjoying the work.

My parents had always taught me to work hard, and my dad was pleased to see me making a quid – while also, in his words, 'getting a degree from the university of life'. He would also pay me pocket money for helping him fix cars in the garage. On reflection, it was more like slave labour than a job – but I'll always cherish the bonding time!

So, by the age of 16, I had accomplished the first step of my financial plan – I had earned some money and, better yet, had been able to save. The next step was to make it grow. At school, we'd been learning about the stock market, so I decided to buy some shares.

I don't remember which company I chose, but I invested £200. I have to say I went into the trade reasonably confident, based on what I'd learned in class – investing in shares was a one-way bet! Oh, how wrong I was. The company tanked. I didn't lose everything, but a big chunk of that £200 – the equivalent of 200 hours in the bakery – was gone. It was a hard lesson in managing risk, and although it felt like a real slap across the face, I was determined to not give up.

It was then I decided to hit the books. Thankfully, I was a bookworm and it wasn't unusual for me, even as a kid, to finish a book a day. (The library could barely keep up with the demand!) Soon, I came across a British company called Abbey National. It had been a building society, but in 1989 went public and started trading on the stock market. The shares were trading for £1.00 each and, I figured, why not put all of my eggs in one basket (again) and spend my entire net worth of £500 on buying 500 shares?

As luck (and a bit more research) would have it, I struck gold this time! I sold those shares for £11 each and made a profit of around £5000, which for a teenager was a hell of a lot of money. But more important than the profit was what that trade taught me. I could use money to make money! I was hooked. For the first time in my life I had actually seen how to make money work for me, rather than having to work for money.

## Finding my golden ticket

Using my profits from that investment, I did what few people from my school had done and enrolled in university. Once there, I knuckled down and gained a Bachelor of Science with Honours in business and finance. That piece of paper was like a golden ticket. Doors began to open.

Before I knew it, I was working in the City of London with some of the biggest investors in the world. My starting salary was around £30,000 a year, which wasn't too shabby for a fresh-faced graduate, but I could see more-experienced colleagues alongside me raking in millions. I realised a whole new world existed beyond what I'd previously known. And once you've seen something like that, you can't unsee it.

From that moment on, I focused my thirst for knowledge on my workmates. I absorbed every bit of wisdom I could from those colleagues who'd made it big. I put my nose to the grindstone and (to mix my metaphors a little) worked my tail off. And you know what? It paid off.

Soon I was working in investment management for a huge global firm where I had a front-row seat to some seriously impressive financial moves. I mean, we're talking about trades worth hundreds of millions of dollars being executed right before my eyes. It was like watching a high-stakes game of financial chess, and I was grateful to be in the game with the master players.

Back then, in the mid-1990s, things were very different from how they are now. These were the days of green monochrome computer monitors and traders on the phone frantically waving their arms around, with not a smartphone in sight. It was like what you'd see in the old Wall Street movies. But I loved it. And I learned some pretty nifty tricks from my colleagues. One of these tricks, for example, was pioneering the use of charts. For the first time, I was seeing this done on a computer screen as opposed to them being drawn out manually. It was a true eye-opener and gave me my first real taste of technical analysis.

## A retirement – of sorts

By 1999, I began to feel a little restless in my job and was craving something more. And, having met an Australian girlfriend, I made a decision to pack up and move to the land Down Under. Thankfully, I had made good money by this point, so I was able to kick back and enjoy some downtime. Essentially, I was living the dream – retired at the age of 29!

I remember reading *Rich Dad, Poor Dad* by Robert Kiyosaki on the plane trip over from the United Kingdom, and it inspired me to start looking at life through a different lens and convinced me to persist with investing beyond the world of trading.

As it turns out, I'm not really the type to just sit around and do nothing. I continued to trade online but, with Kiyosaki's teachings in mind, began to use the proceeds for other forms of investment. Now, I have to say, online trading back in the day was not exactly what it is now. I was pulling cables from the back of my landline phone and plugging them into the computer to get dial-up internet. To millennials, it probably sounds like something from the Stone Age, but it worked!

Before I knew it, I was making enormous profits from the insane 'dot-com boom', which in many ways was like shooting fish in a barrel. I was in a great financial position but, to my own surprise, I still felt unfulfilled – until a chance encounter on a golf course set me on a new and exciting path.

It was a Tuesday and an older chap in my playing group asked me, 'Why aren't you at work?' I responded with, 'Why aren't you at work?' He replied, 'I'm retired', and I said, 'So am I'. This sparked a conversation about how I had built my fortune at such a young age. After explaining my methods to him, he asked me to teach him. And that's when I discovered my passion for financial education.

My new golf buddy would be my first client, but others soon came knocking. At the end of the tax year, my accountant saw the money I was making from trading and wanted to know more. Together, we created a process called 'Cashflow on Demand' (which I also cover later in this book), and I started teaching some of his clients.

Word of this strategy spread quickly and, as my exposure grew, I set about formalising my advice through my Australian financial services license, and growing to become a multi-faceted financial services organisation. For more than a decade, I travelled around the world teaching tens of thousands of investors how to invest successfully, while speaking alongside investors and businessmen such as my childhood idol Robert Kiyosaki, as well as Sir Richard Branson, Tony Robbins and even former British Prime Minister Tony Blair. It's been quite the ride!

Fast-forward to today, and my Australian Investment Education and other businesses have become the go-to sources for investment education and advice, and are helping build financial literacy and confidence in the community. For more than 20 years now, at our very core of values is the relationship with each of our clients, one that is built on trust, care and responsibility.

## WHO THIS BOOK IS FOR

That's enough about me. By now, you're probably wondering how I can help you – after all, that's why you're reading this book.

The good news is that what I've learned over my long journey can be replicated by anyone, regardless of their occupation or financial background. In fact, I sometimes feel people who dropped out of school at 15 make better investors than academics, perhaps because they don't get too caught up in the theory – they simply get started!

The process I outline in this book is simple, streamlined and delivered in clear English. Unlike many in the finance industry, I make an effort to avoid speaking in the kind of code and jargon that often causes eager eyes to glaze over. My simple, 'paint-by-numbers' investing approach can set you free.

You have to be up for it, however. Knowledge on its own isn't power. You need to take action for the results to come. It's rarely you versus life – it's you versus yourself! It's so easy to talk yourself out of doing what's required to be successful in any aspect of life, whether that be investing, fitness or family. Nothing in life happens by accident; you have to make it happen. It's down to you. Knowing where to start, irrespective of your age, and what steps to take next are key.

I have proven you can achieve financial freedom, regardless of where you start.

The strategies, skills and resources provided within this book will not only help you create significant wealth, but also enable you to avoid paying advisors a 'fee for no service'.

# HOW THE BOOK IS ORGANISED

This book is broken into five parts, with the chapters in each part taking you from laying your financial foundation through to developing and implementing your wealth playbook.

## Part I:  Foundations for financial success

In the opening chapters of this book, you'll learn how to open yourself up to a new world of opportunities. It begins by explaining how preconceived beliefs and false narratives may be affecting your ability to build wealth, and how simple changes can lead to exciting new results. Unique tips on goal setting, budgeting and time management will ensure you're well positioned to capitalise on the more complex strategies detailed in later chapters.

## Part II: Transitioning to an investor

Here, you'll begin thinking like an investor. You will become aware of the small, consistent steps that lead to significant financial growth. From the basics of building a savings 'safety net', to more complex tactics around management of debt and risk, the chapters in this part equip you with the knowledge and skills to navigate your financial journey with confidence and precision.

## Part III: The investment universe

This is where you will begin to unravel the mystery behind successful investing. You're first given a detailed checklist to complete before making any investment, which will ensure you maximise the potential for returns while minimising risk. We then dive into a comprehensive exploration of various investment types, including shares, exchange traded funds, managed funds and investment properties. Each option is discussed in detail, allowing you to understand their unique characteristics, benefits and potential risks, and their role in a diversified portfolio.

## Part IV: Money management

Making money is one thing; it's another to keep it. This part introduces you to practical strategies for maintaining your financial health and ensuring you leave a legacy for future generations. Topics such as structuring your investments, superannuation and life insurance are often ignored by novice investors, but here you're given a succinct explanation of why they're so important and how they contribute to a well-rounded financial plan. You'll also find crucial insights into how to deal with a financial crisis and why you need to mark a regular 'date night' on your calendar, even if you don't have a partner!

## Part V: Your playbook

On making it to the end of the book, you are given a comprehensive 'playbook' that brings together all of the knowledge you've acquired. This actionable guide will aid you in journeying through life's various phases while striking a balance between cherishing the present and planning for the future.

Throughout the chapters, I've provided case studies and lesson blocks to help you embed the learnings. I've also included 5-point action plans at the end of each chapter so you can put those learnings into practice. And if you really want to take your financial empowerment to the next level, you can check out the online Success Portal that accompanies this book – just go to wealthplaybook.com.au.

My hope is that this book can be the inspiration you need to achieve exactly what you want from your life. First up, however, you might need to forget many of the things you've been told about money – covered in chapter 1.

# Part I

# FOUNDATIONS FOR FINANCIAL SUCCESS

# Chapter 1

# MONEY STORIES

Just because you heard it, doesn't mean it's true.

Andrew Baxter

From an early age, you'll likely have heard many stories relating to money. Phrases such as 'money won't make you happy', 'the best things in life are free' and 'money is the root of all evil' will no doubt sound familiar.

But in many cases these stories are just that: stories. They are often false truths that have perpetuated over generations, often without being called into question.

Chances are, the money stories you've been told are contributing to the financial situation you're in right now, whether that be good or bad. Some stories make a positive contribution to where you're going in life, whereas others just fuel resentment and negativity.

For example, if you believe that money is inherently bad or that wanting more of it is selfish, you may unconsciously sabotage your own efforts to earn and manage it effectively. On the other hand, if you see money as positive and empowering, you're more likely to naturally attract opportunities to increase your wealth and make better financial decisions.

In this chapter, we'll explore some of the most common money stories and how they might be influencing your reality.

## ANCIENT TEACHINGS

One of the earliest money narratives known to man stems from Psalms 37:11 in the Bible. It reads, 'But the meek shall inherit the earth; and shall delight themselves in the abundance of peace'.

The verse can be understood in various ways depending on a person's religious beliefs and perspectives. Many believe it highlights the importance of humility and patience in life, with the 'meek' considered those who remain passive and gentle, even in the face of adversity. The promise that the meek 'shall inherit the earth' can be seen as an assurance that those who display these virtues will ultimately be rewarded, both in this life and in the afterlife.

However, a less nuanced interpretation also casts a negative light on financial success. In this context, 'meek' is seen as referring to those who do not actively pursue wealth or material success. Over centuries, this has led many to view chasing money as inherently bad or incompatible with a virtuous life.

It's also worth mentioning that persuasive money stories exist in other religions and cultures as well. Buddhist and Hindu teachings, for example, emphasise the importance of non-attachment to material possessions, and in some cases this has led to negative connotations around wealth more generally.

The true intention of such teachings is for individuals to decide, but it's important to at least give thought to their origins before allowing them to shape our beliefs, and ultimately our actions.

## MONEY'S STIGMA

Have you ever stopped to question commonly heard phrases such as 'money is the root of all evil'? A closer inspection reveals that, in many ways, these kinds of sayings are misguided.

Evil people, not money, are the root of all evil. In fact, money is simply an extension of a person's character. If you are morally corrupt and happen to have wealth, you can certainly use that power to cause harm to others.

However, if you are a person of good character, money can be a tool for positive change and making a difference in the world. Ultimately, how money is applied determines whether it causes evil or good, and that depends on the values and intentions of those using it.

---

### CASE STUDY: DISCOVERY VITALITY

In the city of Johannesburg, a South African life insurance company called Discovery has challenged the conventional belief that making money and doing good are mutually exclusive.

Despite operating in a country with a high level of HIV and high mortality rates, the company has managed to provide life insurance for tens of millions of people by taking a purpose-driven approach.

Rather than solely focusing on selling policies, founder Adrian Gore realised the key to helping people live longer and healthier lives was to educate them on how to make better choices.

This led to the company offering its Discovery Vitality program, which provides incentives for healthy behaviours such as eating well, exercising and having regular check-ups. The program has in turn led to Discovery increasing not only the life expectancy of its clients but also its own profits.

Through its innovative approach, the Discovery Vitality program has shown that it's possible to make a positive impact on society while running a profitable business.

Although ample evidence suggests money is not inherently evil, some still hold onto the belief that it can only come at the expense of others. These types of money stories often come from those who are yet to achieve their own financial objectives and seek to excuse their own frustrations by belittling the accomplishments of others.

Throughout your life, you will come across people who can either lift or undermine you, and it's up to you to decide who to listen to and what impact their words will have. Always be aware that some people may be motivated by animosity, envy and jealousy.

Imagine, for example, you're standing with a friend when someone drives past in a luxurious car. What is the conversation that likely follows? Will you assume that it was hard work and smart planning that helped the owner make the purchase? Or is it more likely you will make disparaging comments about the size of their ego, them probably coming from a wealthy family or perhaps earning their money through dishonest or unethical means?

Often overlooked is the fact that, in a capitalist system, financial gain is typically earned by providing solutions to customers' needs or improving their quality of life. Therefore, earning money is a direct consequence of helping society. Unfortunately, the stories we hear about wealth acquisition rarely reflect this positive narrative.

It's essential to understand that creating wealth does not inherently require the exploitation of others. Ultimately, generating wealth can be a force for good, driving innovation and fostering opportunities for positive change within society at large.

## AWKWARD CONVERSATIONS

The way we approach the topic of money is a fascinating aspect of our cultural norms. As children, many of us were taught that discussing money at the dinner table was off limits and even considered taboo.

The reasons behind this are complex and varied, but they are likely rooted in the social stigmas that have historically been attached to discussing financial matters in public. Perhaps one reason for this taboo is the belief that talking about money is impolite or even crass.

Money is often seen as a private matter and discussing it openly may be viewed as intrusive. People may feel uncomfortable discussing the subject because it can highlight disparities in income and wealth, which can be awkward or even embarrassing.

You may even find that the mere act of setting a goal to make money is frowned upon, while almost all other lifestyle goals are encouraged. Say, for example, that you set a goal to be obsessive about health and fitness. Most people would encourage and support that goal, offering any assistance they can provide to help you achieve it.

However, if you expressed a desire to become totally obsessed with making money, the reaction would likely be different. People may view your goal with suspicion, scepticism or even disdain, questioning your motivations and values.

Within your family, consider whether it's time to change these attitudes. Discussions about money should be more open, honest and free from judgement. Make an effort to shift the perception of making money from something frowned upon to something that's admired.

## THE PURSUIT OF HAPPINESS

It's an age-old question: Does money actually make you happy?

Well, many studies have actually looked at this. One of the most famous was conducted by psychologist Daniel Kahneman and economist Angus Deaton, with their research confirming that money does make us happier – up to a certain point. In 2010 when this research took place, that point was a salary of US$75,000. Now, although the study identified that after this point the impact of money on happiness diminishes, it is evident that the common adage 'money won't make you happy' is far from accurate. On the

contrary, this is just another misleading money story that is negatively influencing people's financial decision-making.

And a subsequent 2021 study from the University of Sydney identified that the level of income required to be happy in Australia has
been increasing over the last ten years, while median incomes have
remained about the same. In 'The increasing cost of happiness' the
authors of this study argue this means happiness is not only becoming
more expensive but also moving out of reach for most Australians.

You will often hear people saying they'd rather have a healthy,
balanced life than money. In some ways, that sounds like a sound
philosophy, but why not have both? If you don't have to spend a lot
of time at work to make money, surely that can only be positive?

While I wouldn't change a thing about my modest upbringing, I do
find having the freedom and choice to work on the things I enjoy, while
also spending precious time with my family, is the perfect balance.

It is somewhat true that 'the best things in life are free', but you
can only enjoy those things if you have the time to do so. Playing
with your children might cost you nothing, but you won't be able
to do it as much as you'd like if you're working 60 hours per week.
Entry to the beach is free (in most parts of the world), but if the
weather's bad on your only day off, it won't be much fun!

## IN YOUR DNA?

Another fictional story people often tell themselves is that they
can't become wealthy because they come from a family that has
always struggled with managing money. Well, if you continuously
feed yourself that narrative, you'll end up being right – nothing will
change!

The best approach is to believe in yourself and become the person
who breaks the cycle of financial struggle that has persisted through
past generations by building a stable financial foundation and, eventually, lasting wealth.

After reading this book, and applying the knowledge you've learned, you will realise you have the power to change the trajectory of your family's financial future and establish a new legacy of financial prosperity.

---

## CASE STUDY: KERRY STOKES

Australian businessman Kerry Stokes is a great example of someone who rose to financial success despite his difficult beginnings.

Born John Patrick Alford in 1940, he was adopted out by his unmarried mother into a poor family and grew up in a slum housing area in Melbourne known as Camp Pell. He later dropped out of school at the age of 14.

However, rather than letting his circumstances define him, Stokes worked tirelessly to forge a better future. He went from installing television antennas to becoming the majority shareholder of one of Australia's largest television networks, and eventually one of the richest men in Australia.

In 2000, he told the ABC, Australia's national broadcaster, that his upbringing was one that he wouldn't wish on anybody and described spending time on the streets before finding work.

Today, his net worth is estimated to be in the billions of dollars.

---

What has more bearing on your financial future than your genetics is the social circle you choose to build around you. If you're in an environment where your friends have bad money habits, then there's a very good chance that you will too.

You will often hear the saying 'show me your five closest friends, and I'll show you your future'. The idea behind this is that the people you surround yourself with can have a significant impact on your beliefs, attitudes and behaviour. And, often, when you try to walk down a different path, your peer group will try to pull you back into their way of living because they don't want you to outgrow them.

But you need to find a way to pull yourself out of that rut and focus on your own personal goals. You don't necessarily need to stop being friends with anyone, but you should certainly consider whose lifestyles you want to emulate and from whom you are seeking financial advice.

## THE ULTIMATE MONEY MYTH

Perhaps one of the biggest false beliefs around money is that it's hard to come by. The truth is that more money is in circulation now that there has been at any point in history. As I write this, the US dollar printers will be spinning!

The advent of the internet also means more opportunities exist to get your hands on that money than ever before. Starting your own business and connecting with potential employers, clients or business opportunities is now much easier, and much cheaper.

Once you're making money, it's never been easier to invest. The emergence of online brokerages has made it possible to purchase and trade securities such as stocks and bonds with just a few clicks.

Many of these platforms offer low or no fees, making it more accessible for small investors to engage in the markets. A wide range of online tools and resources are also available to help you make more informed investment decisions.

## CONTROLLING YOUR DESTINY

At this point, I hope you've come to understand that much of the conventional wisdom surrounding money should be taken with a grain of salt. You certainly don't have to sell your soul to the devil to become wealthy.

From this moment on, view financial success as a worthwhile and positive goal. Most importantly, have faith that you can reach your goals regardless of your background or present circumstances.

Next, we're going to start setting some of those goals, but first, here is the five-point action plan I want you to take away from this chapter.

## 5-POINT ACTION PLAN

1. Identify the money stories you have been told throughout your life and question their validity. Consider how they might be influencing your current financial situation – positively or negatively.
2. Recognise that money is not inherently good or bad; it is how it is used that determines its impact.
3. Break the taboo around discussing money by initiating open and honest conversations about finances with those around you, including family and friends. This can help you gain a better understanding of how others approach money and learn from their experiences.
4. Be mindful of the people around you and their attitudes towards money. Surround yourself with people who uplift and inspire you, rather than those who belittle your accomplishments or success.
5. Start creating your positive money story.

## ONLINE RESOURCES

For help in identifying your money stories, access the free resources and training at wealthplaybook.com.au.

# Chapter 2

# GOAL SETTING

If you don't know where you are going,
any road will get you there.
Common paraphrasing, Lewis Carroll, *Alice in Wonderland*

This book will explain how you can achieve absolutely anything you want in life. But first, you need to decide exactly what your 'anything' is. If you're like Alice in *Alice in Wonderland* and 'don't care much' where you want to get to, as the Cat responds, 'it doesn't matter which way you go'.

Ultimately, if you aren't clear on your desired destination, even the best map in the world will be of no use to you. That's why successful people are obsessive about setting goals. Whether it be in business, investing or their personal lives, they like to create a clear game plan that makes success inevitable, rather than leave it to chance.

Now, it's likely that you have set goals in the past and perhaps been disappointed when you didn't achieve them. At the beginning of a new year, you've maybe made resolutions, only to abandon them before they are achieved. If this is the case, you're not alone. Most people make the same mistakes.

The secret to changing this pattern is both simple and profound. In this chapter, I explain how to shift your focus from what you want to achieve to who you wish to become.

# SHAPING YOUR IDENTITY

One of my all-time favourite books is *Atomic Habits* by James Clear. In the opening chapters, Clear explains that simply setting goals isn't enough to help you achieve success. Instead, he argues that the key is to clearly specify the habits you need to adopt to ultimately change your identity. He says that by changing your identity, you are more likely to take the actions necessary to achieve your desired outcomes.

With this in mind, I'm going to outline three different types of goals: achievement goals, habit goals and identity goals. You'll see that they all have their place, but some are more effective than others.

## Achievement goals

Achievement goals focus on very specific outcomes or accomplishments. Here are some examples:

- lose 10 kilograms

- make $100,000 in 12 months through trading

- read a book every month

- learn a new language.

Now, setting achievement goals is better than setting no goals at all. They can definitely provide a sense of direction and motivation. However, they can be a blunt tool for several reasons.

Firstly, they don't address the underlying reasons why you want to achieve them. Sure, you might want to earn $100,000 through trading next year, but why is that an important goal to you? Is it because you want the freedom to quit your job? Do you want enough money to pay private school fees for your children? Or is it your goal because your best friends just paid off their house and you want to do the same?

Exploring the underlying reasons for your goals is crucial because it creates a strong emotional bond with your purpose. Accomplishing goals can be arduous and obstacles will likely pop up along the way, but having a profound personal connection to your objective can provide the motivation to persevere through challenging times and remain focused on achieving the ultimate outcome.

The thought of providing your children with the best possible education, for example, could be emotive enough to pull you back on track during a difficult period. Later in the book, I talk about why it's important not to be emotional when making financial decisions, but in the context of goal setting, you can use your emotions to your advantage.

The other reason setting achievement goals often lead to failure is that they don't make clear the behaviour required to reach them. Losing 10 kilograms, for instance, will require changing your daily routine. That's why it's better to set habit goals.

## Habit goals

The process of setting achievement goals can be compared to steering a car in the direction you want to travel. Habit goals, on the other hand, act as the accelerator, propelling you towards your destination. When you consistently practise good habits, you maintain momentum towards your goals. Conversely, neglecting those habits is like taking your foot off the pedal.

So, what are some examples of habit goals? Well, let's say your achievement goal is to run a marathon. Your habit goal could be to run for an hour every second day. On the alternate days, you could commit to strength training and stretching.

Similarly, if your achievement goal is to invest $50,000 in the stock market, your habit goal could be to save a certain percentage of your income every month. By creating this good habit, you will make consistent, sustainable progress.

A reason it's important to be more focussed on your habit goals than achievement goals is that they are more controllable. For instance, let's say your achievement goal is to win a gold medal at the Olympics. While you can certainly control your training habits and work to improve your skills, your ability to achieve that goal may be impacted by external factors, such as the performance of other athletes or unforeseen injuries.

Another example might be saving money for a deposit on a house. Your achievement goal might be to have enough money saved to buy a home in a certain neighbourhood, but external factors such as changes in the housing market could impact your ability to reach that goal, thereby leaving you disappointed.

By instead setting a habit goal of sticking to a budget and saving a certain percentage of your income each month, you can instead focus your efforts and attention on what you can control. Which house you are then able to buy will depend on those external factors, but you will have done everything in your power to achieve the best possible outcome.

By developing these good habits, they will eventually become so ingrained that they will shape your entire identity. It's at that point, success is guaranteed.


## Identity goals

Identity goals refer to the highest level of goal setting, where you ultimately decide what type of person you wish to become. It is about changing your values and beliefs to align with the identity you desire.

Identity goals can be difficult to achieve because they require a high level of commitment and consistency. That's why it's important to have an emotional connection to the goal. Without it, you will be more likely to give up when the going gets tough.

To create that emotional connection, it's important to think deeply about what it is you're ultimately trying to achieve. For example, aiming to be fit and healthy enough to live a long life with your children is likely to be more inspiring during difficult times than a goal of lifting 100 kilograms on the bench press in the gym.

The identity goal is more powerful than the achievement or habit goals because it becomes a part of your concept of self. The goal is not just about achieving a specific outcome but rather about becoming the type of person who is able to consistently achieve their goals. This identity is an unshakable belief system that operates like a personal operating system.

When highlighting the power of your identity, I tell the story about my dad's response when he was asked why he wouldn't smoke a cigar. He didn't mention specifics about health impacts or his personal morals, but simply said, 'I'm a non-smoker.' When we adopt a specific identity, such as being a non-smoker, it becomes a part of who we are, and our actions naturally align with that self-concept.

As I covered in chapter 1, telling yourself negative stories about your own identity, especially when it comes to money, can be easy. If you think you've never been good with money and never will be, you will be unlikely to achieve financial success. However, if you set a goal of being someone who constantly optimises your income to create a strong financial future for you and your family, and you're prepared to adopt the habits necessary, then you are likely to make that happen.

The following table outlines the difference between achievement, habit and identity goals.

And the following figure highlights how the three types of goal work together, with the achievement goals becoming a pathway to identity goals.

## The Three Types of Goals

| Achievement goal | Habit goal | Identity goal |
|---|---|---|
| Lose 10 kilograms | Exercise for an hour every day | Be a person who is health-conscious, disciplined, motivated and committed to physical improvement |
| Make $100,000 from trading the stock market next year | Follow a strict trading plan and spend 10 hours per week analysing charts, staying informed on financial news and executing trades | Be an analytical, patient, persistent trader with a strong work ethic |
| Read a book a month | Read in bed for 30 minutes every night before going to sleep | Be a focused and intellectually curious person who enjoys learning about new concepts, ideas and perspectives |
| Learn a new language | Listen to podcasts or music in the target language while commuting to and from work | Be someone who speaks another language |

## HOW TO SET GOALS

Now that you know the difference between achievement, habit and identity goals, it's time to make that knowledge work for you. To begin your goal setting process, grab a pen and paper, find a quiet space, turn off your mobile phone and take time to think about what you want from your life and why you want it.

### Begin with achievement and habit goals, and move towards identity goals

If you're new to goal setting, begin by concentrating on specific achievement goals and the habits you need to develop to reach them. This will provide you with a sense of direction and help build momentum.

Your game plan should include actionable steps you can take immediately. Successful business strategist Tony Robbins, a close mentor of mine, often says 'never leave the scene of a decision without first taking a specific action towards its achievement'. Taking immediate action helps with that momentum and makes it easier to follow through with your plan.

If, for example, you have set a habit goal of saving $1,000 every month, then an immediate action you could take would be to open a new savings account where you can start syphoning off that money. Then a process is under way.

The final step is to focus on your identity goals, and work on becoming the person who achieves their desired outcomes in life through consistent, small and intentional actions.

### Revision and maintenance

The process of setting and achieving goals never ends. As you can see in the following figure, you should create a feedback loop, where you are constantly monitoring and adjusting your plan. An action step is followed by an outcome, which can then be evaluated and adjusted. The more laps of this loop you do, the more the circle of growth grows, and the closer you will be to success! This also helps you avoid the opposite feedback loop, where you try something, it doesn't work and so you stop completely.

**The Feedback Loop**

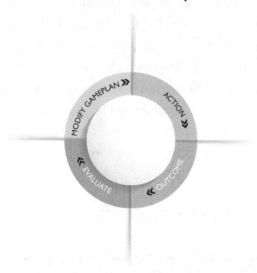

This monitoring can be done on a weekly or monthly basis, and should include a review of all important benchmarks. If you set a goal of saving $1000 every month, did that happen? If not, how far off were you, and why?

It's important to be flexible and revise the plan as needed. For example, if rising interest rates have increased your mortgage repayments, then you may need to scale down your monthly savings target. Your goals never need to be set in stone – flexibility is important.

In chapter 26, I delve into the idea of setting up a regular 'date night' specifically designated for reviewing your financial goals and progress. If you have a partner, this can help you both stay on the same page and maintain a shared vision for your financial future.

## Keeping a journal

One way to monitor and reflect on your progress is by keeping a journal. Writing down your thoughts and ideas about your financial goals can help you stay focused and motivated.

The journal can be as simple as a diary, or you could choose a specialised product like the Money and Investing planner that we provide for our clients, available via our online Success Portal. This will help you develop a crystal clear vision of what you want, and then help you build a step-by-step plan for achieving it.

Goals are essentially dreams with deadlines. Remember, every day counts, and for each day you haven't moved closer to your goals, you've actually moved further away because you have one less day to get there! So, get started and write those goals down on paper so you can begin building your future today!

---

### 5-POINT ACTION PLAN

1. Begin by identifying specific outcomes you want to achieve (achievement goals), and then determine the habits you need to develop in order to reach those goals.
2. Take at least one immediate step towards achieving your goals to ensure you start with strong momentum.
3. Consider what truly matters to you and why you want to achieve these specific outcomes in your life. This will ultimately lead to setting identity goals to solidify your new behaviours.
4. Set up a consistent schedule to review your progress, evaluate the effectiveness of your actions, and make adjustments as needed.
5. Document your progress in a journal to ensure you stay focused and motivated.

## ONLINE RESOURCES

If you would like to get more from your goal setting, we'd love to host you for our free 'Winning The Game' Goals workshop. Visit wealthplaybook.com.au to get access to this session within the members area.

# Chapter 3

# BUDGETING BASICS

Budgeting isn't about limiting yourself; it's about making
the things that excite you possible.

Andrew Baxter

Having an organic farm in Byron Bay has reinforced to me a valuable lesson: for anything to thrive, it must first be pruned. This principle applies just as well to budgeting as it does to growing crops.

Similar to how pruning a fruit tree involves removing dead or unhealthy growth, budgeting requires us to eliminate unnecessary expenses and keep only what really matters. Once we've stripped away the excess, we can begin to channel our energy and resources into cultivating what brings us the most fruit!

Now, you might feel an urge to either skip or skim over this chapter, but I urge you to instead take the time to read it carefully. If you can grasp the ideas here, you'll be well on the way to locking in one of the single most important skills for achieving your goals – self-discipline.

While budgeting may conjure thoughts of restriction, limitation and sacrifice, it is actually one of the most empowering things you can do for yourself. I'll even go as far to say that it can be fun.

Identifying where you can make small adjustments now will ensure that you can enjoy much bigger rewards later. This is what's known as 'delayed gratification', and embracing this concept can set you up for an amazing future.

So, let's start pruning your budget now so you can watch your financial situation begin to flourish.

## FIGHTING YOUR PRIMAL INSTINCTS

From the moment we're born, we're programmed to seek immediate rewards that satisfy our basic needs for food, comfort and attention. These instincts are hardwired into our brains and are essential for our survival and development.

As small children, most of us learn that when we cry, we're comforted with a warm embrace, a soothing voice or food (and often all three). And as we get older, we seek out similar sources of immediate pleasure. Sugary snacks, alcohol, social media and impulse purchases can give us that instant rush we crave.

However, while those things will make you feel good in the moment, that drive for short-term satisfaction will be detrimental in the long term. Sugary snacks will expose you to obesity and disease. Too much alcohol could cause a life-destroying addiction. And impulse purchases will impact how much money you have to invest, thereby keeping you tied to your job for longer.

For these reasons, it's crucial to seek delayed gratification by setting a strict budget that may bring you less pleasure in the short term, but will ultimately lead to greater rewards in the long run. For example, renting a smaller house in a less desirable neighbourhood could allow you to eventually buy the house of your dreams on the best street in town.

Now, although you may know intellectually that delayed gratification is a smart choice, it can still feel like you're going against your very nature when you try to resist the pull of immediate rewards. You may feel frustrated or deprived, and find it difficult to stick to your budget.

However, with practice, you can learn to rewire your brain to think more long term and see delayed gratification as a source of satisfaction and pride, rather than a source of frustration. As shown in the following figure, by focusing on your long-term goals and building good financial habits, you can learn to balance your need for immediate gratification with your desire for a secure and prosperous future.

**Longer Term Goals vs Overall Wealth**

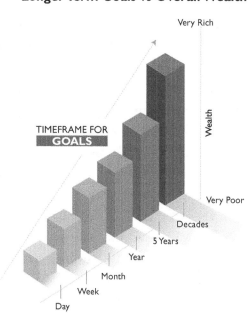

## EVERY PENNY MATTERS

The saying 'look after the pennies and the pounds will take care of themselves' is one you've probably heard many times before. Indeed, it's a piece of financial wisdom that my grandfather passed on to my father, who in turn drummed it into me from a very young age.

Growing up with this mindset allowed me to see the benefits of small savings adding up over time. Don't underestimate the power of removing luxuries such as streaming services, designer clothing and takeaway food from your monthly spend.

## CASE STUDY: THE STANFORD 'MARSHMALLOW EXPERIMENT'

Whilst studying a psychology subject at university, I was introduced to the intriguing 'marshmallow experiment'.

Conducted by Stanford University in 1972, the study involved a group of children who were given either a marshmallow or a pretzel stick, depending on their preference. They were then told they could eat the treat immediately, or wait a period of time and receive two treats.

The researcher would then leave the room and return after 15 minutes to see who took the immediate reward, and who waited for more.

In follow-up studies, it was found that those who chose to delay gratification went on to have significantly higher grades at school, lower body mass indexes and greater overall happiness and success than those who ate their treat straightaway.

Although only a small sample size, the study provides some proof that those who can resist the urge to make impulsive decisions are usually rewarded in the long term.

This might seem obvious to you, but have you ever really committed to making these small sacrifices? Sometimes it seems as though the idea of setting a budget is simply unpalatable!

The process of tracking expenses and cutting spending can feel tedious and overwhelming. And when your friends are out having a good time in cafes, restaurants and nightclubs, it can be difficult not to join them.

Now, not for a moment am I suggesting you should remove all luxuries from your life. If, for example, you have an online shopping habit, I guess you first need to ask why it gives you pleasure and whether it is a positive habit. Your second step is then to allocate an amount in your budget for this. So instead of dropping $400 or $500 on an impulse purchase, if you allow yourself a limit of $150 and stick with that, you are going to be immediately better off. Sounds simple, but very few people keep themselves accountable in that way.

Essentially, budgeting is about prioritising the things that are really important to you. Then, in the long run, you'll actually find you can buy more of your favourite things and enjoy more of your favourite experiences.

## BUY THE CHEAPEST CAR YOUR EGO WILL ALLOW

Let me admit to something: I have a weak spot for cars and I have owned several 'exotics'. However, I was only able to reach that point after first making considerable sacrifices.

When I began my professional journey in London, I made a conscious decision to forgo buying a car and instead relied on public transport. At the time, I could definitely afford my own set of wheels, but I chose to resist the immediate gratification of buying one, and to instead invest in reaching my long-term goals. (And, to be fair, London does have one of the best public transport systems in the world.)

Now, depending on where you live, it could be difficult to forgo a vehicle completely. However, my advice to people is always buy the 'cheapest car your ego will allow'! Ask yourself if you're paying for features that you want or features that you need. This also applies to all purchases – so if you're not that into cars, have a think about other items you might be buying based on ego.

# CASE STUDY: A FOCUSED GOAL VERSUS LACK OF SELF-DISCIPLINE

To highlight the power of strict budgeting, I often tell the story of a former colleague of mine in London who, in the interest of privacy, I will call John.

John had a clear goal – to receive a rent cheque every day of his life. His plan was to achieve this by owning 31 investment properties, providing him with a rent cheque for each day of the month, every month.

Despite being on a fairly standard income, John was determined to achieve his goal – and was willing to make significant sacrifices to make it happen. He gave up his car, lived in a share house and always lived well below his means.

As John's bank balance grew, he bought his first investment property. He was then able to buy one or two investment properties each year by using refinancing and equity from one to buy another.

Today, John is living his dream. He now owns those 31 investment properties (well, actually more) and is in the rare position of receiving a sizeable passive income every single day of the month.

Day to day he can live worry free, knowing that even if a significant drop occurred in the property market, he has enough equity in his houses to well and truly weather the storm.

As a contrast, I will tell you about another former colleague, who I'll call Bill.

Bill lacked self-discipline in various areas of his life, didn't follow a budget and could be quite reckless with his spending. He regularly purchased takeaway and dined at restaurants, spent more on cars than necessary and had a gym membership that he never used.

Bill is a good guy and seems relatively happy in his life, but he is now in the position where he still rents his home and sometimes needs to ask his employer for an advance on his monthly salary because he's run out of money.

It's an example of how spending habits can leave two people on similar salaries in very different financial situations.

## SETTING YOUR BUDGET

This book is all about taking action, so now it's time for you to set your budget.

In the online Success Portal that accompanies this book, I have included a spreadsheet template that will help you lay out all of your monthly expenses. I want you to be very specific and thorough with this – don't leave anything out! Once you have everything laid out, you can then think about where you can make changes and reduce spending to achieve your long-term goals.

Budgeting can seem like a tedious exercise, but it's crucial to building a strong financial foundation. You must also make sure you're regularly tracking your spending to ensure you are staying within the parameters you set yourself. If you don't see your savings account growing each month, then something is wrong!

## 5-POINT ACTION PLAN

1. Identify your long-term financial goals and create a budget to achieve them. Focus on what really matters to you and prioritise those expenses.

2. Practice delayed gratification. Recognise that small sacrifices now can lead to bigger rewards later. Instead of spending money on instant gratification, save that money for a more significant purchase or investment.

3. Keep track of every penny you spend. Monitor your expenses and look for areas where you can cut back on unnecessary spending. Look for subscriptions or memberships you no longer use and cancel them.

4. Set limits for yourself when it comes to spending. Avoid impulsive decisions, and establish a spending limit on things like gambling, dining out or shopping. Be accountable and stick to your limits.

5. Buy the cheapest car your ego will allow. Don't let your ego dictate your spending habits. When it comes to purchasing a car (and other similar purchases), focus on functionality over style, and prioritise reliability and affordability over luxury.

## ONLINE RESOURCES

To help you create a workable budget, we have put together a range of tools to help you build and stay on budget. These tools can be accessed through wealthplaybook.com.au within the members area.

# Chapter 4

# TIME IS MONEY

> Lost time is never found again.
>
> Benjamin Franklin

Benjamin Franklin was a remarkable man who made pivotal contributions to the fields of politics, literature, science and philosophy. But what you may not know is he was also a savvy businessman who recognised the value of time and the impact it has on financial success.

In 1748, Franklin wrote an essay called 'Advice to a Young Tradesman', in which he famously said:

> Remember that time is money. He that can earn ten shillings a day by his labour, and goes abroad, or sits idle one half of that day, tho' he spends but sixpence during his diversion or idleness, ought not to reckon that the only expense; he hath really spent or rather thrown away five shillings besides.

Translated into today's English, Franklin is quite simply reminding us that even if we don't spend much during our leisure time, we are still effectively losing out on potential earnings by not working.

Now, while it is worth emphasising the importance of working hard and earning money, particularly at a young age, I would like to expand further on Franklin's timeless quote and explain how every hour of every day you can be earning income without needing to lift a finger.

## THE IMPORTANCE OF INVESTING EARLY

To make meaningful money while you're sleeping or lying on the beach, you need to make your money work for you. And the earlier you can start this, the better.

Later in the book, I explain how various investing techniques, including Cashflow on Demand (covered in chapter 16), can help you significantly grow your wealth. But the effectiveness of such approaches will depend heavily on one variable: time. The more years you have up your sleeve, the more money you can make.

That might sound obvious, but over many years of providing financial education, I've met countless older people who've told me they never fully understood how time could work for them. Invariably, they wished they'd learned the lesson sooner. As people approach retirement and begin to see that they aren't where they expected to be financially, I see their faces fill with regret.

People can find themselves in such a position for many reasons, ranging from divorce, to failed business ventures, parental responsibilities, and plain bad luck. Regardless of the cause, they will find themselves wondering how they can play catch-up to build the level of wealth they always wanted.

Now, if you're getting older, don't see this as a reason to give up! My advice isn't to not bother starting, but to start immediately! To quote Benjamin Franklin once more, 'Lost time is never found again'. Instead of looking at the past, look to the future and make time your friend.

## THE COMPOUNDING EFFECT

Now it's time to explain how the passage of time can be leveraged to build your wealth. And it all comes down to one of the most powerful concepts in investing: compounding.

Compounding occurs when you continually reinvest what you're making on your money, creating a snowball effect where the return grows exponentially over time. Initially, monitoring the returns will feel like watching paint dry, but if you wait long enough, you'll start to see them really begin to motor.

As an example of how it works, let's say you invest $1000 with an annual return of 10 per cent, and plan to reinvest all returns. After one year, the investment will have grown to $1100. In the second year, not only will the original $1000 investment continue to earn a 10 per cent return, but the additional $100 earned in the first year will also generate a return of 10 per cent, resulting in a total invest-ment value of $1210.

Now, let's fast-forward to 20 years later. With the same annual return of 10 per cent, the initial investment would have grown to an impressive $6727.50. That's a staggering 572 per cent on investment!

### CASE STUDY: THE POWER OF COMPOUNDING ON CONTINUING SMALL CONTRIBUTIONS

To further illustrate the power of compounding, and the benefits of investing early, I will use an example of twin brothers – let's call them Jim and Bob.

On their 18th birthdays, Jim and Bob are given $2000 each from their parents.

Jim immediately decides he'll use the money to embark on an overseas holiday with his friends. He has an amazing seven days, but when he returns every cent is gone.

Bob, on the other hand, is more saving-conscious and invests all of his money into an exchange traded fund (ETF) with an average annual return of 10 per cent. (For more on ETFs, see chapter 15.) Not only that, he also decides to start adding an extra $200 into the ETF each month.

When Jim and Bob turn 30, Jim has nothing and Bob has $61,895.

Impressed by the size of his brother's nest egg, Jim decides to start investing in the same ETF, with a goal of having the same amount of money as Bob by the age of 40.

After doing the maths, he realises if Bob continues investing $200 a month and receiving 10 per cent interest per year, he is likely to have $208,521 by the time he is 40.

This is when Jim is hit with a reality check. With a starting point of zero, he is shocked to learn he would need to invest more than $1000 a month to reach the same figure as his brother by age 40.

If Bob, on the other hand, decided to increase his monthly contribution to $1000 at age 30, he would have $372,397 on his 40th birthday.

In this example, Bob made time his friend. With every day that passed, his investment was growing. Unfortunately, Jim made the common mistake of leaving his run until later and paid a price.

## FINANCIAL DRIFT

So what if you're good at saving, but prefer to keep cash under your bed instead of placing trust in an investment product? Well, it's likely you won't just be missing out on returns, but the value of your money will also depreciate over time.

The $100 you have today is unlikely to have the same buying power as $100 in 12 months' time. This is what we call 'financial drift'.

Financial drift is essentially the opposite of compound interest. In the following figure, you can see that money earning compound interest will grow in value over time, while money left under your bed will fall in value over time because of inflation. For example, if the inflation rate is 3 per cent, then $100 today will only be able to buy goods and services worth $97 in 12 months. This creates a 'cost of inaction' that represents the value lost to inflation *and* the value lost through not investing the funds.

**The Cost of Inaction**

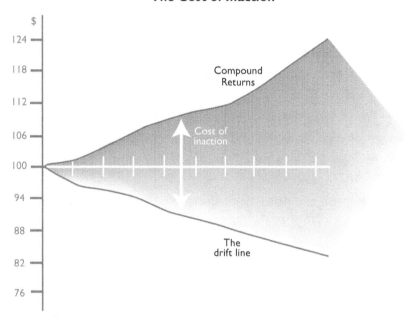

If you keep your money in a savings account, you will earn some interest, but it may still not be enough to keep pace with inflation. Over time, the effects of financial drift can be significant. For example, if you had $10,000 in cash in 1980 and left it under your bed, its purchasing power would have decreased to around $3,500 today due to inflation alone.

However, if you had invested that $10,000 in the stock market, it could have grown to over $160,000, assuming an average annual return of 10 per cent. Therefore, it is important to be aware of the effects of financial drift and take steps to avoid it – and I provide more guidance on what those steps should be in later chapters.

# LESSON BLOCK:
# REAL VERSUS NOMINAL RETURNS

At this stage of the book, it's important to explain the difference between 'nominal' and 'real' returns.

Nominal returns are the actual returns on an investment, before taking into account the effects of inflation.

Real returns, on the other hand, refer to the return on an investment after taking inflation into account. In other words, the actual purchasing power of the return is reflected.

For example, if an investor earns a nominal return of 10 per cent on a stock investment, but inflation over the same period was 6 per cent, the actual return on the investment would only be 4 per cent. (Nominal return − inflation = real return.)

The difference between nominal and real returns can be significant, particularly over long time frames.

The following table shows how this could unfold over a 10-year period if you began with a $100,000 investment. The nominal balances represent the value of the investment based on a 10 per cent annual growth rate without taking into account inflation. The real balances factor in the effects of inflation at three different rates: 2 per cent, 5 per cent and 8 per cent.

| Year | Nominal balance (based on 10% annual growth) | Real balance factoring in 2% inflation | Real balance factoring in 5% inflation | Real balance factoring in 8% inflation |
|---|---|---|---|---|
| 1 | $110,000 | $108,000 | $105,000 | $102,000 |
| 5 | $161,051 | $146,933 | $127,628 | $110,408 |
| 10 | $259,374 | $215,892 | $162,899 | $121,899 |

The table shows that even in a relatively low-inflation environment (2 per cent), the difference between your nominal balance and real balance would be $43,482.

Understanding the difference between real and nominal returns can help you evaluate the performance of your investment portfolios more accurately. You can see, for example, whether an investment is really only keeping up with inflation and not actually providing much in terms of real returns.

It can also ensure you are making informed decisions about the risks and benefits of different types of investments and how they will help you grow real wealth over the long term.

Holding cash may seem like a safe bet, but over a long time frame it will almost certainly leave you with a net loss.

## GET STARTED NOW

The main takeaway from this chapter is that it's important to start investing now, regardless of your stage of life.

Just like a pilot is in charge of a plane reaching its destination, you must take the controls of your life and steer it to where you want to go. A pilot will also constantly make minor corrections to counter unexpected wind speeds. (If a pilot flying between Australia and London waited until the journey was 95 per cent complete before correcting all of the small deviations in the plane's flight path, it could end up in Mongolia!) In a similar way, you must also ensure you're making the relevant adjustments to ensure you're on track to meet your financial goals.

## 5-POINT ACTION PLAN

1. Take the time to understand the concept of compounding and how it can help your investments grow exponentially over time.
2. To make the most of compounding, start investing as early as possible. The earlier you start, the longer your money will have to grow.
3. Avoid financial drift and keep reinvesting the returns on your investments to maximise the compounding effect.
4. Be aware of real versus nominal returns and monitor your investments regularly to ensure they are performing well. Adjust your portfolio where necessary.
5. Be patient and stay committed to your investment plan for the long haul. Compounding takes time to work its magic.

## ONLINE RESOURCES

'Time is money' is way more than a quote, it's the fundamental pillar of wealth creation. To help you understand more on the time value of money, action and the cost of inaction, visit wealthplaybook.com.au and enjoy the free Time Is Money workshop.

# Chapter 5

# THE SIDE HUSTLE

The secret to getting ahead is getting started.
Mark Twain

The idea of having a side hustle has become increasingly popular in recent years – and for good reason. In the age of the internet, it's now easier than ever to offer goods and services to a large customer base, without the enormous start-up costs of the past.

As someone who's been starting successful side hustles since my teenage years, I understand the thrill and empowerment that comes with earning extra income outside of a primary job. Over the journey, I've tried everything from property development to organic farming. It's been a passion that's brought me both joy and financial success – well, at least sometimes!

However, these days, the side hustle is no longer just a trend. For an increasing number of people, having a second or third source of income feels like a necessity. This is because many aren't earning enough in their current roles to support their lifestyle or they're fearful about job security. That's why it's perhaps reassuring to see so many options available for those seeking to diversify.

With a few clicks of a mouse you can start an online store. If social media is your thing, you can earn a full-time income promoting products on Instagram. And let's not even talk about the money that's being made with adult subscription services such as OnlyFans. The options really are varied!

However, before you start thinking about stripping off online, please read and absorb this chapter. I'm a big advocate of the side hustle but, as I will soon explain, it's crucial to choose your venture wisely!

## DO YOU REALLY NEED A SIDE HUSTLE?

You may not be that keen on starting a side hustle for a number of reasons. You could feel too busy with your day job and family to find the time, you may be worried about the start-up costs involved, or you may have a fear of failure.

However, it's important to consider the risk you're taking by relying entirely on your one source of income and not having a 'Plan B'. Be careful of falling into a false sense of security and thinking your job will always be secure. In Australia, we call that a 'she'll be right' attitude, and it can land you in trouble.

Since the early 1990s, we have been very blessed, with most parts of the world enjoying economic boom times. Unemployment rates have overall been low, the stock market has generated strong returns, property has gone up in value and our superannuation balances have been healthy. However, it's good to be aware that conditions can and will change, and becoming complacent could be a big mistake.

It's an unfortunate fact that things don't always pan out the way you want them to. The COVID-19 pandemic also highlighted that anything can happen, and even those people with seemingly secure jobs can find themselves in a precarious situation. During the pandemic and subsequent lockdowns, previously rock-solid industries such as aviation and hospitality suddenly ground to a halt, and employees were given no assurances about when life would return to normal.

Even if you are lucky enough to remain in a stable job for your entire career, there is also the chance of other unexpected events such as medical emergencies or unexpected parenting costs. By diversifying your income streams, you can reduce your reliance on a single source of income, which can be especially important during times of uncertainty.

This might sound like a lot of doom and gloom, and there is a good chance that none of those bad things will happen to you. And if that's the case – brilliant! The money you make from your side hustle can help you pay off debt, save for the future and, most importantly, invest.

So, yes, you may feel too busy to start a side hustle, but it's important to prioritise it even if you can only devote a few hours a month to getting started. You will also find that a side hustle can be immensely satisfying. Having something outside of your 9 to 5 that you're completely in charge of is incredibly liberating.

## CASE STUDY: SUSAN NGUYEN

When the pandemic hit Melbourne in 2020, Vietnamese-born hairdresser Susan Nguyen was forced to close her salon in the coastal suburb of Brighton. Immediately, her primary source of income was gone.

With young daughters to support, Susan decided to spend lockdown learning how to trade markets. It was something she had always wanted to try.

In April of 2020, she signed up to one of my programs at Australian Investment Education and weeks later she was trading. While her friends and colleagues were perhaps at home watching streaming services, she was making money.

By the end of that year, she had made a profit of 60 per cent, which amounted to nearly $70,000. Susan told me starting that side hustle was the best decision she ever made.

By 2021, the young mother was able to scale back her commitment to the salon as her second income stream continued to grow. Wouldn't you do the same if your side hustle had earned you another 74 per cent over the financial year? She was well on the path to achieving her dream of earning income from her laptop, anywhere in the world.

## SIDE HUSTLE OPTIONS

So, hopefully by now you're convinced that a side hustle is something that you should at the very least consider. The next step is to investigate your options.

Obviously, which project you choose will depend on your life situation, skill set and financial position, but to get you thinking, here are some common choices:

- *Amazon selling:* A friend of mine runs a successful program on how to make money from Amazon, but it does take a considerable amount of time to get up and running. You'll need to find your niche, build your product and develop your branding, all of which can take from around 14 to 18 months. It can be a sustainable business, but the lead time is lengthy, so you'll need to bring some resources to the table.

- *Babysitting:* This could be an attractive option if you enjoy spending time with kids and have some experience in childcare. You can also consider offering additional services such as meal preparation or tutoring to make your business stand out and attract more clients.

- *Car detailing:* Many people make a second income by washing, waxing and detailing cars for people who want to keep their vehicles looking like new. This has historically been lucrative for those with a passion for cars and an attention to detail.

- *Event planning:* Planning and coordinating events such as weddings, corporate conferences and parties can be a fun and exciting job if you enjoy working with people. The financial rewards can be great in this industry too!

- *Freelance writing:* Writing articles, blog posts and other content for clients on a freelance basis is something you can do from home at your own pace. It can even lead to a full-time career, allowing you to pursue your passion for writing while making a living. With the demand for quality content constantly increasing, the potential for growth and earning potential is high.

- *Graphic design:* Graphic design is another great option if you have creative flair and enjoy the flexibility of working from home. Many people out there have started side hustles designing logos, business cards and other marketing materials for small businesses and entrepreneurs. Design software is becoming increasingly cheaper and easier to use, making the barriers to entry low.

- *House cleaning:* Offering house cleaning services to busy professionals or families can be a lucrative business if you have a knack for cleaning and organising. With many people leading busy lives, demand is high for reliable and trustworthy cleaners.

- *Landscaping:* Offering lawn care and landscaping services to homeowners and businesses is a tried and tested side hustle. The tasks can be physically demanding, but it's a great way to enjoy time outdoors and get some exercise.

- *Online tutoring:* Video conferencing software means you can now tutor students in a variety of subjects from home. This is a great option if you have teaching experience or expertise in a particular subject. As an online tutor, you can often choose your own hours, making it a perfect fit for those who have busy schedules or enjoy travelling.

- *Personal training:* Personal training is an excellent option if you are passionate about fitness and enjoy helping others achieve their health goals. With the flexibility to set your own schedule and rates, it can be a rewarding and profitable side hustle. As you build your client base and reputation, you could also expand your services and potentially turn it into a full-time career.

- *Pet sitting:* This is a great option if you love animals and have some free time during the day. People are passionate about their pets and are often looking for people to walk and feed them while they're away from home. It can be a great way to stay active and enjoy the outdoors.

- *Photography:* These days everybody has a high-quality camera on their mobile phones, but there is still a demand for professional photographers for events such as weddings, birthdays and family portraits. You can start by building a portfolio and advertising your services on social media.

- *Ride-share driving:* Driving for a ride-share service such as Uber or Lyft allows you to work flexible hours and earn money with your vehicle. This is great if you have time up your sleeve, but don't expect high hourly rates!

- *Social media management:* If you're proficient on social media, consider managing accounts for businesses and influencers. This involves creating and scheduling posts, responding to comments, and growing the audience. Like many of the side hustles already mentioned, the barriers to entry are low because all you need is a computer and an internet connection!

- *Stock market trading:* Over the pandemic, Google searches for terms around stock market investing skyrocketed as people looked at ways to make money during the lockdowns. The problem is that most people don't have the education to do this safely and usually end up losing money. However, if you're prepared to learn, this can indeed be a profitable side hustle. We have many clients who come to us for help and end up creating a substantial second income.

- *Virtual assistance:* These days it is possible to provide administrative support to businesses and entrepreneurs remotely. You will find many clients out there are looking for help with tasks such as scheduling, email management and data entry. You can assist multiple clients at once, which makes it particularly enticing if you have time on your hands!

## WHICH SIDE HUSTLE IS BEST FOR YOU?

Determining the best side hustle for you can be a challenging task. As the following figure shows, the traditional way of thinking about this is to find the intersection between what you enjoy, what you're good at, and how you can make money from it.

**Traditional Thinking**

While it's great to follow your passion, often that won't lead you down the most lucrative path. My advice is to be realistic and find a structured, process-oriented venture with a track record of success over different economic cycles.

To help yourself make the right decision, consider the three factors shown in the following figure (and then covered in the following sections).

**A More Practical Approach**

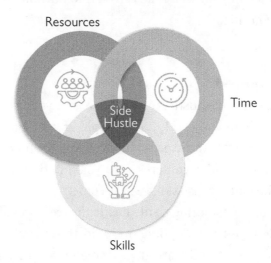

## Cost and resources

How much capital or other resources will you need to launch your side hustle? For example, if you're interested in a side hustle as an Uber driver, do you have a suitable car? Or you may think renovating and flipping a house may be a good option, but do you have the money to cover the significant start-up costs?

In Australia, you currently need a 20 per cent deposit to buy an investment property. Then there are the materials and labour expenses associated with the renovation. By the time you've drawn up plans, received council approvals and done the work, it will also have been many months, if not years, that you've had the house untenanted and not earning you an income.

## Time commitment

Side hustles such as freelance writing, tutoring and ride-share driving won't require much money to get started, but they will demand a lot of your time. It might be tempting to start driving for Uber on your weekends, but be aware that it will take many, many hours to make any meaningful change to your financial position.

It is important to be realistic about the time commitment required for a side hustle and plan accordingly. A venture that takes up too much of your free time can lead to burnout and affect other areas of your life.

## Skills required

To succeed in a side hustle, you need to assess your skills and identify the areas where you excel. For example, if you're a talented artist, you could paint or draw portraits of clients from home using their photographs or video conferencing. You'll find that the more work you do, the better those skills will become.

If you are considering a side hustle that requires skills you don't yet possess, you have options to build those skills. You can take online courses, attend workshops or read relevant books and blogs to learn more about your chosen side hustle. Additionally, networking with other professionals in the industry can help you learn from their experiences and get tips on how to improve your skills.

In my experience, you will need either money, time or skills to begin a successful side hustle, but you don't need to tick all three boxes. The most important thing to do is assess which of those resources you have available to you and create a bulletproof plan of attack to move forward.

## HOW TO GET STARTED

Once you've chosen your side hustle, it's time to take action! However, while it's tempting to jump in headfirst, this approach can lead to costly mistakes and setbacks. Instead, take the time to learn about your industry, hone your skills, and develop a solid plan.

This means eliminating distractions and staying focused on the next steps. It's also important to consider the risks and returns associated with your project. While the potential for profit is certainly enticing, it's crucial to avoid falling victim to scams or predatory practices.

You also don't want your pursuit of a side hustle to take over your life, to the detriment of your relationships and work–life balance. So also consider how you will manage your time and resources to effectively balance your side hustle with your primary job and other commitments. Make a plan for setting goals and establishing a sustainable routine.

When people come to me for help starting a second income stream, I stress the importance of not cutting corners. It is great to be able to fast-track your success, but it must always be in a safe and sustainable way.

### 5-POINT ACTION PLAN

1. Assess your current financial situation and identify potential risks of relying on one source of income. Consider the possibility of unexpected events, such as job loss or medical emergencies, and how diversifying your income streams can help mitigate these risks.
2. Determine if a side hustle is right for you. While it may seem challenging to find time for a side hustle, consider how even a few hours a month can help you earn extra income and provide a sense of financial security.

3. Research potential side hustle options that align with your skills and interests. Freelance writing, online tutoring and e-commerce are all examples of viable options that can provide a sustainable source of additional income.

4. Evaluate the start-up costs and time commitment involved with each potential side hustle. While some options, such as freelance writing, require little to no investment, others, such as e-commerce, may require higher upfront costs.

5. Create a plan for how you will manage your time and resources to effectively balance your side hustle with your primary job and other commitments. Consider setting goals and establishing a routine that allows you to make progress towards your side hustle while maintaining a healthy work–life balance.

## ONLINE RESOURCES

Identifying a side hustle which is both a fun thing and financially lucrative can be a real game changer. For help identifying yours, visit wealthplaybook.com.au and check out the free workshop.

# Chapter 6

# YOUR TEAM

Don't be the smartest person in the room – if you are,
you're in the wrong room!
Andrew Baxter

Growing wealth requires more than just financial literacy. You also need a level of humility and the willingness to seek help from those who specialise in areas where your expertise may currently be lacking.

While you should definitely educate yourself to a level where you can manage most of your own affairs, never be afraid to enlist the services of professionals who are recognised as experts in their field.

Think of yourself as the conductor of your orchestra. You are ultimately in control, but to succeed you need the right people playing the right instruments. And just like you wouldn't ask a violinist to play the trumpet, don't ask a tax accountant to choose your stocks. Each expert should work within their specific area of expertise to create a beautiful symphony of success.

My friend Robert Kiyosaki, author of *Rich Dad, Poor Dad*, is an excellent example of someone who's successfully embraced this approach. By bringing together specialists in tax, real estate, law and sales, he's been able to amass enormous wealth. To use his words, 'The richest people in the world look for and build networks; everyone else looks for work.'

Now, I know what you're thinking. This all sounds great in theory, but how do you find the right people to join your team? And how much will it cost? Never fear. In this chapter, I explain which experts you need, how to pick the right people, and the tricks to avoid paying them more than you should.

## TAX COMES FIRST

Even before you get serious about investing, you should find a good personal tax accountant. While it may be tempting to try to save money by working out your income and expenses on an Excel spreadsheet and doing your own annual return, the reality is it'll probably end up costing you more. Missing important lodgement dates will incur penalties and it's likely you'll be unaware of potential tax deductions that a good accountant will find.

I discuss investment structures in more detail in chapter 21, but an accountant can also help you set up the most appropriate structure for your business or finances. This can involve setting up companies, trusts or self-managed superannuation funds, while ensuring compliance with tax laws and regulations. Proper structuring can help minimise tax liabilities and maximise financial opportunities.

However, it's important to know that not all accountants are created equal. Some may simply act as collectors for the tax office and add no value to your return, while others may try too hard to maximise your claim and land both of you in legal trouble! It's important to find someone who will work hard for you without crossing into dangerous territory.

So where should you start looking? My advice is to be very careful choosing someone who you've seen advertised on websites or social media. While their selling points can appear very alluring, it can be impossible to know whether they have the ability to deliver.

Usually the best way to find a reliable, trustworthy accountant is via referrals from friends, family or colleagues. Pay particular attention to suggestions from people who are on a similar pathway or playing field as you. For example, if you run your own plumbing business, it's worth seeking advice from other tradies, as opposed to a shop assistant or teacher.

Once you've been referred to an accountant, it's important not to dive in head first and appoint the first one you meet. Arrange a meeting with the person to ensure you are able to connect with them. You should also evaluate their fee structure and main areas of expertise to ensure they are the right fit for you.

A good tip is to avoid hiring generalists who claim to be experts across many areas. Instead, seek out specialists. It is definitely possible for an accountant to 'do everything', but rarely can they do everything well. If you are starting an online business, go to someone who specialises in internet start-ups. Similarly, for estate planning, make sure your accountant genuinely understand your goals and objectives (and your lawyer as well, which I cover in the next section).

I will be honest, though – I have learned my lessons the hard way. I've had some absolutely terrible accountants. And, regardless of whether they're sole practitioners or employed by a big firm, they can be hard to spot. That's why personal referrals can be so valuable and why it's crucial to carefully screen potential candidates.

One technique I suggest is asking the accountant for a list of every tax deduction they consider relevant to your field and financial position. This request places the responsibility on them to show some initiative and prove they're taking your account seriously.

You might be surprised at what expenses you are able to legitimately claim as part of your tax return. For instance, if you're a tradesperson, you may be able to claim expenses associated with owning a Rottweiler if the dog helps to guard expensive tools and machinery on your premises.

If you work from home, you can claim a portion of your internet usage, utility bills, cleaning expenses and repairs to your home office furniture and fittings. However, claiming these expenses may create later tax implications when you go to sell the property – so, again, get good advice.

## LAWYER UP

Having a good quality lawyer on your team is extremely important, regardless of the type of business you are in. Many people only
consider hiring a lawyer when they are in trouble, but this can be
a short-sighted or reactionary approach.

A good lawyer can add significant value to your business, helping
you navigate legal issues and avoid costly mistakes. For example,
if you are active in the property space, a good conveyancing special-
ist can be absolutely crucial.

I discovered this firsthand when a property I'd sold sustained
storm damage after the contract went unconditional, meaning both
parties are obligated to proceed with the transaction, but before
the settlement date. The buyer argued that because we were still
in the settlement period, I should pick up the repair bill. However,
at the time, I had an excellent conveyancer who was quickly able to
point to a clause in the contract showing it was the buyer's responsibility to have insurance during this period. Her good work saved
me almost $60,000.

In addition to providing legal advice and expertise for any specific
issues you may have, a good lawyer can also help you stay up to date
with changing laws and regulations that may affect your business,
and advise you on compliance matters.

In some cases, they can also help you attract investors or secure
financing. Investors and lenders often want to see that a company
has taken the necessary steps to protect its assets and minimise legal
risks, and having a lawyer can demonstrate that you are taking this
seriously.

## FIND A COACH

When it comes to seeking advice around where to invest your money,
many options are available. Depending on your circumstances and

game plan, you can turn to traditional consultants, such as financial advisors, financial planners or stockbrokers. However, while these professionals can be important, their scope is often too narrow. It may be more beneficial to engage a money coach, who can help you navigate the bigger picture and provide a holistic approach to managing money.

A money coach can offer advice on not just investment strategies, but also budgeting, debt reduction, retirement planning and estate planning. They can help you identify your financial goals, assess your risk tolerance, and develop a customised plan that takes into account your unique circumstances and priorities. In other words, a good money coach won't just tell you what to do. Rather, they will empower you to make the financial choices that are right for you and your situation.

This will be particularly helpful for those who feel overwhelmed about how to start their financial journey. The money coach can even help you find those good accountants and lawyers that can help you along the way. They can also help you avoid the pitfalls that often come with bringing that team together.

Keep the following in mind when searching for your money coach:

1. Make sure they hold an Australian financial services license; otherwise, they are operating illegally – not a good start.

2. Avoid advisors who are part of a large dealer group, because you will be tied to products that typically only are provided by that dealer group, rather than having access to a wider choice.

3. Look for a money coach who is also an educator, and can help you understand and make decisions for yourself rather than simply selling you products.

4. Make sure you read the documents provided carefully, paying particular attention to fees, charges and, most importantly, commission rebates for referring your business to third parties. This can be especially important if you are looking at property investing.

## LESSON BLOCK: FIVE THINGS TO LOOK OUT FOR WHEN BUILDING YOUR TEAM

When undergoing the process of building your support crew, it is important to be aware of the common problems that can arise.

Here are five common pitfalls I've seen over my many years of engaging external advisors:

1. *Bad advice:* If your advisor is suggesting you do something that's risky, immoral or illegal, you should end the relationship immediately. Beware of recommendations to invest offshore to avoid paying tax. It rarely ends well.

2. *Unlicensed advice:* Be cautious when seeking investing advice from people who operate outside their lane – such as accountants, for example, who may not have a financial services licence. While they may be experts in tax and structural decisions, they may not have the necessary expertise, authorisation or qualifications in investing to provide sound, legitimate advice.

3. *Fee creep:* Always make sure that you're getting the value you're paying for. If fees are increasing without any corresponding improvement in service, consider looking for another provider.

4. *Relationship slippage:* If you feel like your advisor is taking your business for granted, it may be time to find someone who values your business and is committed to helping you succeed.

5. *Dealer group ties:* Beware of financial planners who are associated with large dealer groups, because they will usually only recommend their own financial products, even if they're not necessarily the best product in the market. Consider working with smaller firms that can offer a more tailored approach to your financial planning needs.

## REMAIN IN CONTROL

Meeting with your advisors can be intimidating because they will ultimately know more than you – that is, after all, why you have hired them! But you should always remember that you are the master and they are the servant. They work for you.

Instead of letting them dictate the plan, clearly communicate your goals and ask what they will do to help you achieve them. Don't be afraid to ask questions and speak up if something doesn't make sense to you.

It's also important to establish open lines of communication with your advisors. Don't wait until something goes wrong to contact them. Regular check-ins and updates can help prevent issues from arising and keep everyone on the same page.

You should also never be afraid to ask your advisors to come together into the same room if you are dealing with a major decision or problem. For example, when my wife and I had some complex structuring matters to address, we arranged a meeting with both our accountant and lawyer. After explaining what we were looking for, we left them to work it out and returned an hour later. To our delight, they came up with a clear game plan that took into account both tax effectiveness and asset protection. It was evident that they had worked together seamlessly, and the bill for their advice was more than worth it, considering the amount of money that was saved.

Also consider how your requirements will evolve over time. As your investment strategies and structures become more sophis-ticated and specialised, so too will the expertise and advice you require from your team.

## DON'T BE AFRAID TO SWITCH

If your advisor isn't meeting your expectations, don't hesitate to seek other options. It's common to feel trapped in a professional

**Your Team**

| | BASIC | INTERMEDIATE | ADVANCED |
|---|---|---|---|
| Accounting Advice | Personal Tax Return<br>Super Contribution | Company Accounts<br>Company Tax<br>BAS/GST<br>Family Trust Accounts | Accounting Inter-Entity Efficiency<br>Succession Planning |
| Legal Advice | Will<br>Conveyancing | Company Incorporation<br>SMSF Establishment<br>Family Trust | Family Trust Utilisation<br>SMSF Evolution<br>Legacy<br>  Will<br>  Memorandom of wishes<br>  Binding death nomination |

relationship with an accountant, financial planner or stockbroker, especially when your money is involved.

But switching to a new provider can be a relatively straight-forward and stress-free process. Each industry has guidelines in place to ensure that clients can transfer their business without fear or complications.

So, when it comes to making a change, do not let fear (or laziness) hold you back. A fresh set of eyes can be very helpful when trying to achieve your financial goals. As an example of this, I had a policy of rotating accountants every four years. This ensured I always had someone who was eager to demonstrate their value and ensured fees weren't constantly creeping higher.

## BE PREPARED TO SPEND

While I have stressed the importance of ensuring you're getting value for your money, it is also worth remembering that a good advisor can save you much more money than you're paying them. On occasion, I've paid significant fees for lawyers, but still seen a value added return on that spend of multiples of the cost.

By putting the right person into bat to deal with a substantial challenge, you can potentially see a difference of hundreds of thousands of dollars in the outcome. So, while it's important to consider the cost of an advisor, it's also essential to consider the value they can bring and the potential return on investment.

And remember – if you're the smartest person in the room, you're in the wrong room!

## 5-POINT ACTION PLAN

1. Start by identifying the professionals you need to help you achieve your financial goals. These may include a personal tax accountant, a financial planner, a lawyer and a money coach.

2. Seek referrals from friends, family or colleagues who have used these professionals and can vouch for their quality of service. Avoid hiring professionals who advertise online unless secondary sources can vouch for their ability. Client testimonials can often provide valuable insight.

3. Take the time to screen potential candidates and evaluate their expertise and fee structure. Avoid hiring generalists who claim to be experts in everything and instead seek out specialists in your specific field.

4. When interviewing potential accountants, ask them for a list of every tax deduction they consider relevant to your field and financial position. This will help you evaluate their level of expertise and ensure they are taking your account seriously.

5. Hire a lawyer before you think you need one. A good lawyer can add significant value to your business by helping you navigate legal issues and avoid costly mistakes. Look for a lawyer who specialises in your specific industry or area of need.

## ONLINE RESOURCES

For help building your team, learning more on how to pick the right advisor and the process for engaging them visit wealthplaybook.com.au and enjoy the free team building resources.

# Chapter 7

# POCKET MONEY

Earning is learning.

Andrew Baxter

The chapters in this part are all about the fundamental principles of financial success. Now it's time to put them into practice in your daily life. And one of the best ways to start is by establishing a pocket money system for your children, if you have them. Think of it as a small-scale practice run before you set up your own wealth-building strategy!

Now, even if you don't have little ones, this chapter is essential reading. By highlighting some real-world examples, it will help consolidate the ideas outlined in part I of the book. There will be lessons here for people of all ages.

It has to be said, pocket money is a subject close to my heart. As the father of five, it's something I've had a lot of experience with. And while each family's financial situation is unique, you can't underestimate the power of teaching a child money management skills from a young age.

The way we introduce pocket money can have a significant impact on our children's financial future. The process is not just about giving them cash on demand or setting spending limits. Instead, it's about teaching them the value of money, and budgeting, saving and spending responsibly. By doing so, you can help them develop the skills and habits that will set them up for life.

## FAMILY VALUES

In chapter 1, I outlined how the money stories you hear and learn can have a significant impact on your financial behaviour. This also applies to managing your children's pocket money, because your own upbringing and personal beliefs are likely to shape your approach.

Having grown up in a low-income household where pocket money wasn't simply handed out, I have a dim view of giving children money for doing nothing. Research would suggest that this can create a sense of entitlement and lead children to believe that money is just something to be expected.

On the other hand, giving children pocket money as a reward for assisting with household chores can help them develop a sense of responsibility and independence. By earning their own money, they learn the value of hard work and saving and can connect the dots between effort and reward.

My mother was a big proponent of this philosophy. She would incentivise me to do chores around the house, such as cleaning the windows or doing the washing up. She even gave me a breakdown of the payment in a little brown envelope, much like a pay slip.

We have adopted a similar approach in our household by implementing a weekly allowance system for each child based on their age. For example, an eight year old receives $8 a week, a six year old receives $6 a week and so on. This money is earned by helping out with small tasks around the house. We also offer bonus payments for any 'extra' tasks the kids pick up through the week – such as mowing the lawn or taking the rubbish out. This provides them with a sense of financial independence.

Overall, my children seem to be big fans of this pocket money system and we have noticed it changes their habits for the better. Even the youngest of my kids follow their siblings' lead by helping out because they want to, not just for the financial reward!

## CASE STUDY: SAVING YOUR BACON

As soon as your children start receiving pocket money, you may notice a shift in their spending and saving habits. To illustrate this point, let's use my son Jack's behaviour as an example.

Jack is a huge fan of bacon and has taken it upon himself to cook it for the family on Sunday mornings. At first, he would carelessly throw an entire packet of bacon on the hot plate each time. However, since learning that the cost of a packet of bacon is equivalent to nearly two weeks' worth of his pocket money, he has become very conscious of how much he uses.

Of course, we have never made Jack actually pay for the bacon, but just the understanding of the cost has led him to adjusting his behaviour.

Similarly, we have seen changes in the spending habits of my eldest daughter, Charlotte, who 'earns' the most money of our kids because she takes on the extra task of picking up her horse's manure in the paddock every week.

After her first few paydays, she was very excited and decided she was going to buy a new horse riding helmet. However, upon realising the particular one she wanted would cost the equivalent of about 30 weeks' work, she decided the helmet she already had was perfectly fine!

We were proud of Charlotte for arriving at this conclusion herself, and it proved a valuable lesson about the relationship between effort and reward. It was great to see her asking the ultimate buying question: do I need it, or do I want it?

## PART-TIME JOBS

The idea of kids having part-time jobs can be controversial and polarising. While many people believe a child's younger years should be spent playing and doing homework, other people hold alternate views. Perhaps mine stems from my working-class background.

From a very young age, my dad wanted to teach me the importance of learning skills and working hard by having me help him fix cars in our garage. Instead of sitting on the couch on Saturdays, I would be out there with him and would get paid five pounds for my efforts. Looking back, while the five quid was awesome, this father–son time was precious and something we both look back on with happy memories.

As I grew older, I started to look for ways to get a pay rise and scored that proper first job at a bakery in my village (as I mention in the introduction to this book). Despite the modest salary of one pound per hour, I managed to save quite a bit of money for someone of my age.

I recall once working an exhausting 96 hours in the week leading up to Christmas to save up for something I really wanted. My boss was so impressed he even gave me a £4 bonus to make it an even £100. Once I had enough for that thing I wanted, guess what? I decided I didn't want it because I knew how much work had gone into saving that much money. Again, it came down to that important question of whether I needed it or wanted it.

More important than the cash, however, were the life lessons that are learned by working at a young age. It's a valuable lesson for children today. Working at a place like McDonald's, for example, may not be glamorous, but it can provide invaluable training and experience in repeatable systems and customer service.

However, all of that said, it is also important to strike a balance and ensure that children don't overwork themselves and miss out on opportunities at school.

## FINDING A BALANCE

While teaching children about money is crucial, it's equally important to allow them to enjoy being kids. Children possess natural curiosity and love to explore the world, so we should encourage their exploration without too many restrictions – or, worse, looking through our sometimes cynical adult lenses.

Pocket money should serve as a token of appreciation for their help around the house. It's essential to be mindful of the way we give instructions, however, because it can negatively impact the relationship we establish with our children. We don't want them to view money as the sole motivator for completing tasks.

Adopting a heavy-handed approach with younger kids seldom works, particularly when they're already tired from other activities. Therefore, it's critical to respect their time and energy and recognise when they need a break and some pure and simple playtime.

Similarly, we should avoid being too stringent regarding our children's spending habits. In our household, I tend to manage our investments, given that's my area of expertise, while Emma manages our household. (With five kids, I reckon I have the easy job!)

One area in particular that Emma handles far better than me is making sure the kids enjoy plenty of colour in their lives. On occasion, she'll allow our kids to dip into their savings jar to purchase treats from the local store, which they love. It's important to apply this principle to our own lives and remember to have fun and enjoy some colour along the way.

## SETTING UP YOUR PLAN

Now it's time to sit down and map out a pocket money system for your household. I recommend setting up a table that has the name of the child, their standard base salary (based on their age) and then any extra task they might carry out. While this may seem a little over the top, it's a very useful exercise and should be carried out in parallel with the managing of your household budget.

The 'base salary' is paid for basic everyday tasks, including washing up, clearing the table and making beds. The extra task will be something a little more demanding and specialised, such as cleaning windows, vacuuming the car, picking fruit or sweeping up leaves.

At the end of each week, give each of your children a 'payslip' that shows how much they earned and a breakdown of what the payments were for. The following table illustrates how a plan may look for a family of four.

### Pocket Money and Chores Payment Example

| Child | Weekly base salary | Extra task | Total payment |
|---|---|---|---|
| Cameron (age 14) | $14 | Mowing the lawn weekly (+$5) | $19 |
| Harriett (age 10) | $10 | Feeding the dog daily (+$4) | $14 |
| Rebecca (age 8) | $8 | Taking the rubbish out daily (+$4) | $12 |
| Fred (age 7) | $7 | Watering the tomatoes twice per week (+$3) | $10 |

At the end of the year, consider implementing a 'money match' system in which you simply tally up what the children saved throughout the year and 'match it', or a percentage of it, based on your household budget. This exercise emphasises the concept that money can grow through interest or investment returns.

Depending on your children's age and level of comprehension, you may also want to set aside a portion of their investment returns as 'splurge money' that can be spent on whatever they choose. This strategy ensures that only profits or investment returns are used for lifestyle expenses, not the principal or savings themselves – one of the ultimate money tips of life.

Ultimately, the way in which you implement your personal financial system is entirely at your discretion. And it's worth noting that the objective of this chapter is to provide sound financial guidance, rather than parenting advice! If you don't have children, you can still note how the basic principles can be applied to your own spending. This includes reminding yourself how long you had to work to achieve the money you're about to spend, asking yourself if you need or want the items, and allowing yourself some colour and splurge money – out of your investment returns.

## 5-POINT ACTION PLAN

1. Consider your own upbringing and personal beliefs when managing your children's pocket money.
2. Introduce a pocket money system for your children based on their age and encourage them to earn it by completing small tasks around the house.
3. Teach your children the value of hard work and saving by showing them the cost of the things they enjoy.
4. Encourage your children to take on part-time jobs, when they're old enough, to further develop their skills and work ethic.
5. Use pocket money as a teaching tool to instil financial literacy and habits early on in life. By doing so, you can set your children up for a financially successful future.

## ONLINE RESOURCES

For more detailed information on pocket money strategies, get access to the free pocket money workshop at wealthplaybook.com.au.

# Part II

# TRANSITIONING TO AN INVESTOR

# Chapter 8

# START WITH A SAFETY NET

Expect the best, plan for the worst,
and prepare to be surprised.
Denis Waitley

Now that we've laid the foundations for financial success, it's time to focus on the small, consistent steps that will help grow your wealth. But before we get to the really fun stuff, let's install a safety net that will catch you in the event of an unexpected fall. Life is full of surprises and you must be prepared for any scenario.

Although my family is now fortunate enough to be in a financially secure position, unexpected expenses have in the past left me reeling. Shortly after graduating from university, I was on the brink of tears when the gas boiler in my newly purchased, run-down Victorian terrace house suddenly blew up.

I had stretched my finances thin to buy the property in a less-than-desirable part of London and had very little money left to rectify the situation. It was the dead of winter, and I was suddenly without heat or hot water. Not fun!

British Gas already had an enormous backlog of repair jobs to tackle, and the only way to fast-track my repair was to pay an extra £200. Against my instincts, I paid the premium, only to discover upon the repairman's arrival that I would need to fork out an additional £1500 to replace my entire heating and hot water system.

That was a substantial sum back then, and I recall feeling sick to my stomach. Although British Gas had plans where the cost (and interest) could be added to my quarterly gas bill, my wise father had always warned me against taking on that kind of debt.

In the end, I managed to cobble together the funds from various sources, which meant that I also had to reprioritise my money. The new mattress that I needed had to wait another six months, but the experience taught me a harsh lesson. Having an emergency fund is critical for those inevitable moments when things go wrong.

## HOW TO START AN EMERGENCY FUND

To get started, open a new bank account that is separate from your regular day-to-day accounts. This will prevent you from 'accidentally' using the funds in this account for other expenses.

Once you've done that, you can arrange for a direct deposit to be made into the account on a regular basis, until it has the required amount of money in it. This can be done by transferring money from one of your existing accounts. By automating the process, you can ensure that a set amount of money is consistently being added to your emergency fund each week, fortnight or month, as needed.

Keep in mind that this money should not be considered an investment asset that is expected to generate a return. While it's a bonus if you can find a bank that provides decent interest rate on savings accounts, the primary goal is to have a readily available source of funds that can be accessed quickly when required. If you have a home loan, a good idea could be to set up the account as an offset account so that those emergency funds are reducing your interest payments.

The best part about creating this glass jar of money to break in case of an emergency is that it will have taught you great habits and discipline, and these in turn will help you become a more regular saver.

## How much do you need?

Once you've created that emergency fund, the next step is to determine how much money you need to set aside. Your initial goal should be to save enough money to cover one month of your expenses. Hopefully after the earlier budgeting chapter, you have established what that amount is. Obviously, the more you can cut those unnecessary expenses down, the less money you have to save!

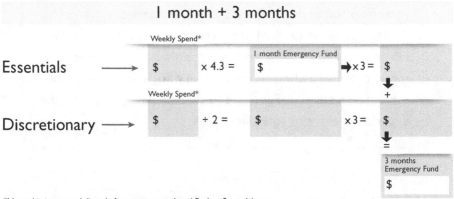

*Note this is sourced directly form your completed Budget Spreadsheet.

For people who usually live week to week, saving enough to cover expenses for a month without income will seem like a steep hill to climb. If that is the case for you, then consider some of the tips from chapter 5 on side hustles to see if you can speed up the process. Depending on your circumstances, a second job or side project may feel like a real drag, but the peace of mind you'll receive by having those extra savings will be well worth it.

After achieving your one month emergency fund goal, the next objective is to aim for saving enough to cover three months of expense. This will get you to the point where you are covered in the event of a significant setback that requires a more extended recovery period.

Go to wealthplaybook.com for more information on how to calculate the right amount for you.

---

## CASE STUDY: PANDEMIC LESSONS

The COVID-19 pandemic highlighted the importance of having an emergency fund.

According to a survey conducted by YouGov for Forbes in April 2021, almost 40 per cent of those with emergency funds had to use them during the pandemic, with 73.3 per cent using up at least half of the fund and 29 per cent depleting it entirely.

The pandemic resulted in many people losing their jobs and income, while their living expenses continued. Although governments provided assistance, it was usually not immediate, and not everyone was eligible. For those without an emergency fund, the experience was very stressful indeed.

---

### When to use your emergency fund

It's important to create a list of situations where it is acceptable to dip into your emergency fund. And let me be clear: you need to be sure they're genuine emergencies. These situations may include covering living costs during unemployment, unexpected medical expenses, the cost of repairs due to weather damage, veterinarian bills, vehicle repair bills or surprise tax bills, although the ATO can offer payment plans.

Remember, the purpose of an emergency fund is to avoid accruing debt during tough times and to alleviate the stress of scrambling to find money when unexpected expenses arise. You want to be able to focus on addressing the emergency, not worrying about how to pay for it.

At times, you may be tempted to dip into your emergency fund for non-emergency expenses, but I strongly advise against it. Attending a friend's wedding overseas or buying an expensive suit for a job interview aren't emergencies. If it can wait, save up for a few weeks and use those funds instead.

Think about the hard work and discipline that went into saving the emergency funds and don't fall back into old habits of spending money on things you don't need.

## LESSON BLOCK: IDENTIFYING AN EMERGENCY EXPENSE

Here is a three-point checklist to help you identify if the expense is an emergency:

1. *Is the expense absolutely necessary?* Before using your emergency fund, assess whether the expense is essential for your wellbeing, safety or ability to earn income. Examples of such expenses include medical emergencies, urgent home repairs or job-related needs like replacing a broken-down car. If the expense is not essential, consider alternative ways to address the issue, such as cutting back on discretionary spending or creating a separate savings goal for the desired purchase.

2. *Will you regret using the funds for this in the future?* Consider the long-term consequences of dipping into your emergency fund. Ask yourself if you will regret using the funds for this expense later, especially if another urgent need arises in the future. Emergency funds should be reserved for genuine emergencies, so it's important to think about whether you are compromising your financial security by tapping into these savings. If you believe you might regret the decision later on, it's likely not a true emergency and you should explore other funding options.

3. *Is an alternative available to deal with this challenge without using the emergency fund?* Explore all possible alternatives to address the financial challenge at hand. For example, can you negotiate a payment plan for medical bills or home repairs? If the lack of funds is only a short-term issue, can you secure a low-interest loan from a family member or friend, or consider using a low-interest credit card as a last resort? (You would then need to quickly pay off the balance of this credit card.) If viable alternatives are available that don't require using your emergency fund, pursue those options first. Remember, the emergency fund should be a last line of defence for genuine emergencies, so exhaust all other avenues before tapping into it.

By carefully evaluating each expense against this three-point checklist, you can ensure that your emergency fund remains intact for genuine emergencies and helps maintain your financial stability during unexpected crises.

And remember, if you do decided to dip into it, you will have to replenish your emergency fund to build it back up again!

## KEEP TRACK OF YOUR SPENDING

As time goes on and your life changes, it's likely your monthly expenses will increase, so it's important you top up your emergency fund accordingly. With five children, two horses and an assortment of other animals, my family's household expenses have increased significantly since it was just Emma and me. However, we continue to adhere to our principles and ensure we make the necessary adjustments to how much we keep in our emergency fund.

It is really important to understand that even as your circumstances change – and perhaps even if you seem to be awash with plenty of spare cash – you should persist with the same financial processes. Success in life is about continuing to master the basics.

## 5-POINT ACTION PLAN

1. Open a new bank account specifically for your emergency fund. This will help you keep your emergency fund separate from your regular accounts and prevent you from accidentally using it for other expenses.

2. Calculate your monthly expenses and set a goal to save at least one month's worth of expenses initially. After that, aim to save enough to cover three months of expenses.

3. Set up a direct deposit or transfer from your regular accounts to your emergency fund account. By automating the process, you can ensure that a set amount of money is consistently being added to your emergency fund each week, fortnight or month.

4. Make a list of genuine emergencies that you can use your emergency fund for, such as unexpected medical expenses, unemployment, weather damage, veterinarian bills, vehicle repairs or surprise tax bills.

5. Keep track of your spending to ensure that you're not using your emergency fund for non-emergency expenses. Remember that the purpose of an emergency fund is to avoid accruing debt during tough times and to alleviate the stress of scrambling to find money when unexpected expenses arise.

## ONLINE RESOURCES

For help on calculating and then setting up your emergency fund, check out the free Safety Net Workshop at wealthplaybook.com.au.

# Chapter 9

# UNDERSTANDING DEBT

With debt, it's the good, the bad and the ugly.

Andrew Baxter

My father has always offered very clear advice on taking on debt: as long as you owe money, someone else owns you. It's an attitude that's shared by many folks of his generation, who tend to value saving and living within their means above borrowing to buy more.

As a result of having those words drummed into me from a young age, I've also been debt adverse throughout my life. Overall, this attitude has saved me a lot of stress and kept me financially secure.

However, there have definitely been times when I've missed out on investment opportunities as a result of my reluctance to owe money. Many successful investors have used debt to their advantage, particularly during times when the cost of borrowing is relatively cheap.

In your own life, you've probably heard advice from both sides: those who tell you debt is the devil, and those who tell you to borrow as much money as the banks will give you! As always, the right approach falls somewhere in the middle.

Debt can be a monster that controls your life, but it can also be your friend. In this chapter, we'll explore the difference between good and bad (and ugly) debt, and how the former can help you reach your financial goals.

# WHAT IS GOOD DEBT?

Good debt is a type of debt that's taken on for a productive purpose and has the potential to generate long-term benefits. As opposed to debts on credit cards and personal loans, good debt usually has a low interest rate and can realistically be paid off on time! I cover some examples of good debt in the following sections.

## Your mortgage

One of the most common examples of good debt is a mortgage on a primary residence. A home not only is a place to live, but also usually appreciates in value over time. As you pay down the mortgage, the equity in the home increases, which can be leveraged to access additional capital if needed.

As long as the mortgage payments are manageable and the property is well maintained, taking out a mortgage can be a wise decision.

## Investment loans

Loans to purchase investments such as stocks, bonds or real estate can be a form of good debt if these investments have the potential to generate long-term returns.

For example, a rental property can generate passive income and appreciate in value over time. The rental income generated can be used to pay off the mortgage and other expenses associated with owning the property. Various tax benefits are also available, because the owner can claim the interest payments on the investment loan as deductions against their income.

### Education loans

Education loans can be considered a type of good debt because they're an investment in your future earning potential. By investing in education and acquiring knowledge and skills, you can secure higher paying jobs and better opportunities for career advancement.

Depending on where you live, the government may provide education loans at a significantly discounted interest rate.

## WHAT IS BAD DEBT?

Now, let's be very clear: debt can indeed be downright dangerous and can lead to a cycle of financial hardship that will be very hard to break. This type of debt is what we refer to as 'bad debt'.

So, what qualifies as bad debt? Well, several types fall into this category, covered in the following sections.

### Credit cards

While credit cards and store cards may seem like a convenient way to make purchases and spread out the payments over time, they usually come with high interest rates that can cause your debt to quickly spiral out of control.

People often make the mistake of only making the minimum monthly payment on these cards, which results in the accumulation of interest on their debt and drags out the repayment process for years.

While credit cards can be handy for collecting rewards such as frequent flyer points, it's best to avoid them unless you are very disciplined when it comes to paying off the full balance each month.

### Personal loans

Personal loans can also be a form of bad debt. While they may be necessary for emergency expenses or to consolidate other high-interest debts, they should be approached with caution. Personal loans often come with high interest rates and fees, and the repayment terms can be difficult to manage for those living pay cheque to pay cheque.

Where possible, you should avoid taking out personal loans for lifestyle purchases, such as cars, bikes, boats, caravans and jet skis. While these treats may seem like a good idea at the time, they are not likely to increase in value and can quickly become a financial burden.

## Buy now, pay later schemes

Buy now, pay later schemes allow customers to make purchases and pay for them in a set number of instalments, often with no interest (within the repayment period). The customer receives the product upfront and makes repayments over a set period of time, typically through automatic payments linked to a debit or credit card.

It all sounds too good to be true and, in my opinion, it is. While such platforms advertise '0% interest', they usually charge fees for late payments. And when the schemes first began to grow in popularity around 2020, initial studies found that one in five users was failing to pay on time. Even if you are meeting the deadlines, you will likely face fees for monthly account-keeping and payment processing.

While credit cards at least have credit checks and limits, the buy now, pay later industry hasn't been as well regulated and the same level of due diligence isn't required before customers sign up.

In my opinion, the early iterations of buy now, pay later services amount to predatory lending. The marketing usually targets young people by offering an easy way to spend money they don't have. And, unfortunately, social media has fuelled a surge in demand for the schemes, with people feeling increasing pressure to buy the latest clothes and gadgets that their friends are showing off online.

In the opening quote for this chapter, I refer to 'the good, the bad and the ugly' of debt. If a mortgage is the 'good' and a credit card is the 'bad', then buy now, pay later is the 'ugly'.

The following figure summarises the different types of good debt and bad debt.

| Good Debt | | | Bad Debt |
|---|---|---|---|
| Your Mortgage | | | Credit Card |
| Investment Loans | | | Personal Loans |
| Education Loans | | | Buy now, pay later schemes |

## LESSON BLOCK: AVOIDING 'BUY NOW, PAIN LATER'

Keep the following in mind when considering buy now, pay later services:

- It's easy to overspend when you're not spending your own money.
- Fees for the establishment of your account, late payments, monthly account-keeping and payment processing can add up.
- Signing up to multiple buy now, pay later services can make it hard to keep track of repayments.
- Late payments can appear on your credit report and affect your ability to borrow money for important purchases – such as a house – in the future.
- Buying a product through the traditional 'lay-by' system (where available) can be a cheaper and safer choice. (In this system, you similarly pay for the product in instalments, but only receive it when it is paid off. Such systems usually come with no additional fees.)

## DEBT CONSOLIDATION

If you're serious about moving forward as an investor, eliminating bad debt is crucial. One strategy that could help you do this is called *debt consolidation.*

Debt consolidation involves combining all of your high-interest debts into a single, more manageable loan that has a much lower overall interest rate. For example, a personal loan can be used to pay off credit card debt, which typically carries higher interest rates.

To illustrate my point, let's look at two tables, which highlight the difference between having four separate debts and one consolidated loan.

### Before debt consolidation
The following table outlines total interest paid on four separate debts (various credit cards and a personal loan).

**Before Debt Consolidation**

|  | Balance | Interest rate | Monthly payment | Loan duration (months) | Total interest paid |
|---|---|---|---|---|---|
| Credit Card A | $5,000 | 18% | $250 | 24 | $989 |
| Credit Card B | $3,000 | 22% | $150 | 26 | $771 |
| Credit Card C | $2,000 | 20% | $100 | 25 | $453 |
| Personal loan | $10,000 | 12% | $300 | 41 | $2,225 |
| Total | $20,000 | | $800 | | $4,438 |

### After debt consolidation
The next table shows how this total interest can be reduced by consolidating the debt into one low-interest personal loan.

**After Debt Consolidation**

| | Balance | Interest rate | Monthly payment | Loan duration (months) | Total interest paid |
|---|---|---|---|---|---|
| Consolidated loan | $20,000 | 9% | $800 | 28 | $2,232 |

You can see that by keeping four separate debts, you would pay a total of $4,438 in interest payments. However, by consolidating the debt into one loan, shopping around for a lower interest rate and paying off the balance a little quicker, the total interest paid would be only $2,232. That's a saving of $2,206.

Now, using this strategy does have some potential downsides. Firstly, after clearing your credit cards, you may feel tempted to start using them again. It is crucial that you don't!

Secondly, by applying for the personal loan or balance transfer credit card, the lender will perform a hard inquiry on your credit, which will likely lower your credit score in the short term. However, in the long run, it should be worth it if you're meeting all of your repayments.

## CLEARING NON-DEDUCTIBLE DEBT

Earlier, I described the mortgage on your house as 'good debt', but you should still try to pay it down as quickly as possible. This is because home loan costs are not tax-deductible, and having non-deductible debt makes wealth creation difficult.

To illustrate, let's consider a scenario where you pay a tax in Australia at a marginal rate of 47 per cent. Say you also have a home loan of $500,000 with an interest rate of 4 per cent. To cover the annual interest plus principal payments of $29,000, of the earnings taxed at your top marginal rate, you must earn $52,727 before tax. That will be a substantial burden as you attempt to achieve long-term financial goals, so it's preferable to get rid of it as soon as possible.

The key to this is making extra payments where possible. In the case of a $500,000 mortgage, increasing your annual repayments from $29,000 to $40,000, for example, would reduce the length of your loan from 30 years to under 18 years, assuming the interest rate was stable. As you can see in the following table, you would also save $160,000 in interest.

**Early Mortgage Elimination**

| Loan amount | Interest rate | Annual repayments | Total interest paid | Time taken to pay off loan |
|---|---|---|---|---|
| $500,000 | 4% | $29,000 | $367,000 | 30 years |
| $500,000 | 4% | $40,000 | $207,000 | 17 years, 9 months |

What makes this particularly powerful is that you will now have the remaining 12 years of that loan term to invest that $40,000 into other investments, including your superannuation. If you let that $40,000 invested every year for 12 years compound at an interest rate of 6 per cent, you'll end up with an additional $732,881 of assets.

I hope this example has shown why paying off your non-deductible debt should be one of the first steps in your wealth creation strategy. Surprisingly, many of my clients fail to give priority to paying off their home loan and it usually impedes their progress significantly.

## DEBT RECYCLING

A more advanced method of paying down your non-deductible debt involves what's known as 'debt recycling'.

Now, it's important to note that debt recycling is a relatively complex concept and I don't recommend trying it unless you fully understand how it works and are comfortable with the risks involved. However, if done properly, it can be a very powerful tool.

At its most basic level, debt recycling is about transferring your non-deductible debt of a home loan into a deductible debt of an investment loan. You do this by taking out a loan against the equity in your home to invest in assets such as shares or managed funds, which generate income and offer the potential for growth over time. Those returns are then used to reduce your non-deductible home loan. *Note:* great care and caution should be taken here in regard to selecting the specific investments to generate these returns and avoid unnecessary levels of risk.

The goal for the end of the first year is to increase your investment loan by the same amount that you've paid on your home loan and reinvest that increased amount. Ideally, you then repeat this process each year until your investment loan entirely replaces your home loan.

To show you what I mean, let's use the example of John and Sarah, who are both in their early forties and are exploring options to pay off their home loan quickly and accumulate wealth. Their home is valued at $800,000 and they have a remaining mortgage balance of $250,000. Their financial advisor recommends debt recycling as a strategy.

Leveraging the equity in their home, John and Sarah secure an interest-only investment loan of $100,000 and channel it into the stock market, opting for a managed fund with promising long-term returns.

In the first year, the couple's investment income and tax savings amount to $5,000, which they add to their routine principal mortgage payments of $8,000 to pay $13,000 off their mortgage, reducing the outstanding balance to $237,000.

Note that this $5000 in investment income and tax savings is the return after subtracting the cost of the interest-only payments on the investment loan. To keep this example simple, I've also only included the principle mortgage payments on John and Sarah's home loan. Of course, in reality, they would also need to be repaying the interest charged on the home loan. (For example, the annual repayment on a $250,000 loan with a 5 per cent interest rate over 30 years would be just over $16,000.) However, this strategy is about focusing on how much the principle of the home loan is being reduced by, and increasing the investment loan by the same amount.

During the second year, they boost their investment loan by $13,000 (the sum they repaid on the principle of their home loan) and replicate the process. This time, they earn an investment income of $5,650. Coupled with their $8,000 cash flow, it allows them to pay $13,650 off their mortgage, leaving a balance of $223,350.

For 15 years, John and Sarah persist with this approach, annually utilising the investment income and $8,000 cash flow to decrease their mortgage while simultaneously reinvesting the same sum in their share portfolio.

By the conclusion of year 15, they have completely paid off their mortgage, replacing the non-deductible debt with a tax-deductible investment loan. The following table breaks down the progression over the 15-year period.

If John and Sarah had just made $8,000 in mortgage payments each year without using debt recycling, they would still have a mortgage of $130,000 after 15 years. They would also be without their share portfolio, which after 15 years could be earning a healthy passive income.

When done properly, debt recycling is an effective double-pronged strategy that allows you to pay down your mortgage while also building an investment portfolio. The impact on your financial position over a long period can be significant.

However, for it to work, you will need to have willpower, discipline and patience. It will be tempting to use your new investment income and tax savings on a 'want' like a holiday or new car. You may also be discouraged from continuing the strategy if you have a few years of low investment returns. Remember to play the long game.

### Debt Recycling Example

| Year | Mortgage size | Investment loan | Investment income (calculated at 5%) | Regular mortgage payments (principal payments) | Total mortgage payments (regular + investment income) |
|---|---|---|---|---|---|
| 1 | $250,000 | $100,000 | $5,000 | $8,000 | $13,000 |
| 2 | $237,000 | $113,000 | $5,650 | $8,000 | $13,650 |
| 3 | $223,350 | $126,650 | $6,333 | $8,000 | $14,333 |
| 4 | $209,017 | $140,983 | $7,049 | $8,000 | $15,049 |
| 5 | $193,968 | $156,032 | $7,802 | $8,000 | $15,802 |
| 6 | $178,166 | $171,834 | $8,592 | $8,000 | $16,592 |
| 7 | $161,574 | $188,426 | $9,421 | $8,000 | $17,421 |
| 8 | $144,153 | $205,847 | $10,292 | $8,000 | $18,292 |
| 9 | $125,861 | $224,139 | $11,207 | $8,000 | $19,207 |
| 10 | $106,654 | $254,346 | $12,167 | $8,000 | $20,167 |
| 11 | $86,487 | $263,513 | $13,176 | $8,000 | $21,176 |
| 12 | $65,311 | $284,689 | $14,234 | $8,000 | $22,234 |
| 13 | $43,077 | $306,923 | $15,346 | $8,000 | $23,346 |
| 14 | $19,731 | $330,269 | $16,513 | $8,000 | $24,513 |
| 15 | $0 | $350,000 | $17,500 | $8,000 | $17,500 |

## Debt recycling risks

In particular, consider the following risks when thinking about a debt recycling strategy or discussing it with your money coach or financial advisor:

- The investments made using the borrowed funds may not perform as expected, or may even decline in value, which could result in a loss. For this reason, I teach my clients how to insure their shares.

- Interest rates on investment loans can fluctuate and if rates increase, the cost of borrowing will increase, which may impact the profitability of the investment.

- Economic factors such as a recession or a stock market crash can impact the value of investments, potentially resulting in a significant loss.

- The tax benefits associated with debt recycling can be complicated and there may be changes to tax laws that could impact your strategy.

- If the investments made using the borrowed funds are not easily liquidated, it may be difficult to access funds when you need them.

## SEEK PROFESSIONAL HELP

Without doubt, debt can be an important tool in today's world, but for the reasons explained in this chapter, it's important to seek advice before you dive in.

Financial experts can provide valuable insights on the different types of loans available, and as I discuss in more detail in chapter 21, they can help you set up a financial structure that ensures you're receiving the most tax benefits available to you.

Most importantly, an expert can ensure you're not taking unnecessary risks – a topic we'll explore further in the next chapter.

## 5-POINT ACTION PLAN

1. Recognise the differences between good debt (mortgages, investment loans, education loans) and bad debt (credit cards, personal loans, and buy now, pay later schemes). Aim to minimise bad debt and focus on good debt that can help generate long-term benefits.

2. Avoid the 'ugly' debt: stay away from buy now, pay later schemes that may seem attractive but often come with hidden fees and encourage overspending. Instead, save up for purchases and consider lay-by systems as a safer alternative.

3. If you have multiple high-interest debts, consider consolidating them into a single, more manageable loan with a lower interest rate. This can save you money on interest payments and help you pay off your debt faster.

4. Prioritise paying off non-deductible debt such as your home mortgage as quickly as possible. Make extra payments when you can to reduce the loan term and save on interest payments.

5. If you're comfortable with the risks and understand the process, explore debt recycling as a way to transform non-deductible debt into tax-deductible investment debt. This advanced strategy can help you pay off your mortgage faster while building an investment portfolio.

## ONLINE RESOURCES

Understanding Debt Recycling and how it works is a key breakthrough but is not suitable for everyone. To help you understand this concept more, check out the workshop at wealthplaybook.com.au.

# Chapter 10

# RISK AND REWARD

Financial success doesn't come from how much you
make, but from how much you keep.

Andrew Baxter

To achieve financial success through investing, you need to focus on more than just making profits. You must also be able to protect your capital. Markets can turn quickly and any money you've made can be wiped out in a flash.

Now, every investment involves some degree of risk – it's almost impossible to avoid it completely. However, the common belief that making more money requires more risk isn't always true.

In fact, one of the key investment strategies detailed later in this book has been proven to provide higher returns than Australia's leading share market index, while also exposing investors to less risk. (This strategy uses exchange-traded options – see chapter 16 for more details.)

Throughout history, the best investors have been masters of safeguarding their wealth, and this is a skill that can only be acquired through proper education. As Warren Buffett once said, 'Risk comes from not knowing what you're doing.'

## CASE STUDY: WHEN THINGS GO WRONG

Some examples of 'force majeure' or 'black swan' events include:

- *The dot-com bubble:* The dot-com bubble of the late 1990s saw many investors pour money into internet-related stocks, hoping to cash in on the 'new economy'. However, when the bubble burst in 2000, many of these companies went bankrupt and investors lost billions of dollars.
- *September 11:* The financial fallout from the attack on the World Trade Center towers and the Pentagon on September 11, 2001 was immense. The US stock market closed for four trading days, marking the longest shutdown since the Great Depression.
- *The global financial crisis:* Anyone who owned shares or had a large superannuation balance at the time won't have forgotten the financial crisis of 2007. In the United States, the stock market plummeted, with nearly $8 trillion in value wiped out between late 2007 and 2009. Home values and retirement accounts were also hit hard.
- *The COVID-19 pandemic:* The COVID-19 pandemic profoundly impacted global markets, causing unprecedented volatility and economic downturns. Lockdown measures disrupted supply chains, while businesses and industries faced severe challenges. Central banks and governments implemented stimulus packages to mitigate the crisis, leading to a partial recovery, but long-term consequences were unavoidable.

## UNDERSTANDING RISK

In the simplest terms, 'risk' is the potential for the value of your investments to move away from expectations. Understanding the events or factors that could cause such moves is crucial before you enter any financial commitment.

In my experience, the greatest risk is the one you're not aware of. So, before you begin your investing journey, let's consider the types of risk you might encounter:

## 'Force majeure' risk

In the world of investing, there will always be the chance of what's known as a 'force majeure'. The French term translates as 'greater force', and refers to an unforeseen and uncontrollable event. In investing, this type of event is one that can significantly impact financial markets, investments or the ability of parties to fulfil their financial obligations.

These extraordinary events may include natural disasters, wars, terrorist attacks, pandemics or government interventions.

You may also hear these types of events being referred to as 'black swan' events – a term coined by Nassim Nicholas Taleb in his 2007 book *The Black Swan: The Impact of the Highly Improbable*. Taleb argues that 'black swans' are more common and influential than most realise, and that investors should develop resilient systems that can withstand them.

## Inflation risk

In times of inflation, the purchasing power of money decreases, meaning each unit of currency buys less than it did before. This can have significant impacts on your investments.

Among the worst assets to hold during times of high inflation are fixed-interest investments such as bonds (which I cover in chapter 17). These lock you into a specific return over a set period and, if inflation rises, the fixed return doesn't change. As a result, the real return after accounting for inflation diminishes.

For instance, a five-year bond with a 3.5 per cent interest rate may seem like a good investment when inflation is low, but with inflation at 7 per cent, you're left with a net real loss of 3.5 per cent each year.

An alternate way of looking at this is in five years' time, taking into account the annual net loss after inflation, for every $100 you invested, your purchasing power would be equivalent to around $82.50. The following two figures highlight this idea in more detail, first showing what $100 in 1970 is equivalent to today in terms of purchasing power, and the second showing how inflation has increased the price of a cup of coffee over time.

**$100 in 1970, adjusted for inflation**

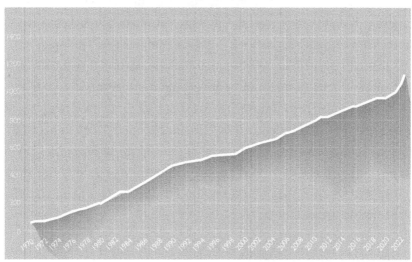

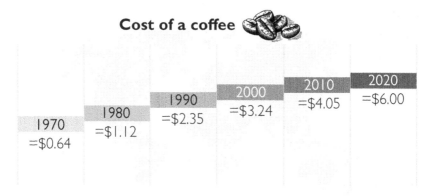

Cost of a coffee

| 1970 | 1980 | 1990 | 2000 | 2010 | 2020 |
| --- | --- | --- | --- | --- | --- |
| =$0.64 | =$1.12 | =$2.35 | =$3.24 | =$4.05 | =$6.00 |

In inflationary periods, tangible assets such as real estate typically perform well, because inflation often coincides with a robust economy. Gold has historically been a popular investment during these times, although in recent years, its ability to perform better than inflation has not always been the case.

In the stock market, some companies perform better than others. Those that can easily pass on price increases to customers, such as Australian road toll operators who adjust tolls based on the Consumer Price Index (CPI), are somewhat shielded from inflation risk.

On the other hand, companies that compete primarily on price, rather than product quality or differentiation, may face challenges.

## Interest rate risk

If you have a large mortgage, you'll know all too well the impact rising interest rates can have on your hip pocket. However, it's not just homeowners who feel the effects.

Investors across all other asset classes need to be aware of how rate fluctuations in either direction can impact their returns. For example, if you borrowed funds to invest in the stock market, the cost of servicing that debt could exceed your returns when rates increase.

It's for this reason that many investors opt for fixed interest rates, even if they're higher than the current variable alternative. The same option is available when you take out a mortgage, but you need to be aware that you risk paying much more interest if variable rates fall!

For investment property owners, rising interest rates can be partially counterbalanced by increased tax deductions. As your annual interest payments rise, you can claim more against your overall income, providing a greater level of stability.

## Volatility risk

In investing, volatility refers to the degree of fluctuations in prices over a given period. In general, higher volatility implies greater risk, while lower volatility suggests reduced risk. A good investor will always consider an investment's volatility when constructing their portfolio.

It's important to understand that some investments are naturally more volatile. For example, cryptocurrencies and small-cap stocks can experience major value fluctuations, making them a better fit for investors seeking aggressive growth.

However, these types of investments come with considerable risks and may not be ideal for those looking for a stable portfolio. 'Blue-chip' or more stable stocks such as Apple and Coca-Cola, on the other hand, are unlikely to give you explosive growth, but typically provide more earnings predictability. (See chapter 14 for more on these types of stocks.)

The two common ways to quantify volatility are 'standard deviation' and 'beta'. Standard deviation calculates how much an investment's returns deviate from its average return over a specific period, while beta measures an investment's sensitivity to overall market movements by comparing its volatility to that of a benchmark index, such as America's S&P 500.

Another measure available is the VIX index, which gauges the expected volatility in the S&P 500 over the next 30 days. Also known as the 'fear index' or the 'misery index', the VIX can be a useful indicator of market sentiment and uncertainty.

Although the VIX index itself is not directly tradable, investors can use it as a risk-management tool and trade VIX-related financial products such as futures, options and other exchange-traded products to speculate on or hedge against changes in market volatility. This approach, however, requires a higher level of education and skill to execute effectively. (See chapter 16 for more on these products.)

## Liquidity risk

Liquidity refers to the ease with which an asset can be bought or sold in the market. Essentially, it measures the number of buyers and sellers available. Blue-chip stocks, for example, typically have high liquidity, with millions of shares being traded daily. However, when dealing with smaller or more speculative assets, liquidity can become a risk.

The issue of liquidity can also affect property investments. Unlike stocks, where traded volume is transparent and easily accessible, assessing liquidity in the property market can be more challenging. Buyers should consider the appeal of a property to a broad market, rather than investing in unique or niche properties that may be difficult to sell later on. Buyers should also be aware that even properties with high appeal will take weeks or months to settle and for funds to be accessible – unlike shares, which can be sold and funds accessed immediately.

During times of financial crisis, liquidity can become a significant concern. For instance, during the global financial crisis, many investors in mortgage funds found themselves unable to withdraw their cash due to the illiquid nature of the assets being held. This led to losses and, in some cases, insolvency for those involved.

## Counterparty risk

In any financial transaction, it's essential to be aware of counterparty risk, which involves thoroughly understanding who you're dealing with and the potential risks associated with them. For example, if you're looking for equity partners in a property development project, make sure you know your partners well. Failure to do so can result in significant financial losses.

In the stock market, verify that the companies or entities you deal with have proper licensing and a reliable track record. Similarly, when it comes to property or property development, make sure you're dealing with the right entity.

Some companies may have complex structures with multiple subsidiaries, and you could end up entering a contract with a subsidiary that has no assets or financial backing, putting your investment at risk.

## Time frame risk

It's essential to ensure that your investments align with your expectations and financial goals in terms of time horizon. For example, if you plan to draw on your investment in five years to transition into retirement or pay off debt, you need to have assets with a matching time frame. Otherwise, you may find yourself unable to access the funds without paying significant penalties or experiencing other challenges.

Matching the time frame of your investment or trade to your capital needs is vital. This is especially true when dealing with fixed-term investments, such as term deposits or bonds.

Be cautious with capital-guaranteed products, because they may guarantee your capital only at maturity, not if you redeem early. This means that if you need to exit your investment before its maturity date, you might not be able to access your funds without incurring losses or paying penalties.

It's crucial to thoroughly read and understand the terms and conditions of your investment products, particularly when it comes to capital guarantees and early redemptions. By aligning your investments with your financial goals and time frames, you can avoid potential pitfalls.

## Property risk

You have numerous aspects to consider when managing risk in property investments. First and foremost, ensure your insurance policies are up to date. This includes building and contents insurance if it's your home or just building insurance if you're a landlord. Landlord insurance is essential to protect the value of your asset and to cover situations such as tenants not paying rent or causing property damage.

Income protection is also essential, particularly for negatively geared properties. In the event that something happens to you, income protection can help cover the costs associated with servicing the property. Mortgage insurance is another standard consideration to ensure peace of mind when using borrowed money.

Be cautious with strategies that involve *cross-collateralisation* (where an asset that's used as security for an initial loan is then used as security for a second loan), because they can lead to significant financial issues if not managed correctly. Understanding the risks associated with buying off-plan properties is also crucial. The property market can fluctuate, and the value of a property may change during the construction phase. Seeking legal advice and carefully reviewing contracts to ensure your interests are protected is essential.

## CASE STUDY: PROPERTY RISK

In a real-life example from the property market, one of our clients' brothers purchased two investment properties in Port Hedland during the mining boom.

At the time, properties were expensive due to the astronomical income generated from the shortage of accommodation in the area.

He bought two very basic shacks for $1.2 million each, which rented out for several thousand dollars a week, driven by market forces at the time.

However, as the mining industry slowed down, the value of these properties dropped to around $400,000 each. The ramifications were serious – creating the need for the owner to tip in more cash or sell and realise the capital loss, neither of which at the time were appealing, while the rent on the properties was a fraction of what it had been at the time of purchase.

This case demonstrates the importance of considering both income and yield perspectives when investing in property, because market forces can change drastically, impacting property values and returns.

## HOW TO MANAGE RISK

Managing risk is crucial in any investment strategy. As highlighted at the start of chapter 8, you should always expect the best and prepare for the worst. When the outcome inevitably falls somewhere in the middle, you can be adequately equipped to respond effectively.

Just as you wouldn't wait for a house fire to occur before purchasing home and contents insurance, it's vital not to wait for a market crash to determine your course of action. Proactively implementing risk management measures is key to safeguarding your investments. I cover some essential considerations in the following sections.

### Diversification

As the age-old saying advises, it's unwise to put all your eggs in one basket. Instead, you should spread your investments across various asset classes, sectors and geographic regions to minimise the impact of individual underperforming investments.

When investing in the stock market, consider buying a diverse range of individual stocks or use exchange-traded funds (ETFs) that track a specific index. ETFs allow investors to gain exposure to an entire market segment, benefiting from its collective performance while mitigating the risks tied to individual stocks.

### Stop-losses

Using stop-losses is another essential risk management technique when investing in shares. A stop-loss is essentially an automatic instruction to sell an asset when its price reaches a specified level or 'pain threshold'!

For example, if you purchase a stock for $10 a share, you can set a stop-loss at $9.50 to ensure you can't lose more than 5 per cent on the trade. Once the market price of the share hits $9.50, a sell order will automatically be executed.

This strategy helps you manage your losses more effectively and prevents you from holding on to losing positions in the hope that the asset's price will eventually recover.

## Structuring

Structuring is essential when it comes to risk mitigation. The primary goal is to ensure that if anything goes wrong, the risk is contained within a 'bomb-proof box', protecting your other assets and investments from any negative consequences. This can be achieved by carefully considering the structure of your investments and loans, as well as who is the guarantor of those loans.

To establish the right structure for your investments, it's vital to seek expert advice rather than relying on generic online searches. Consult with a professional who specialises in asset protection and structuring to ensure your hard work and efforts are safeguarded.

By expecting the best while planning for the worst, you can minimise the impact of any poor decisions or unfortunate events on your overall financial stability. Proper structuring allows you to remain accountable without jeopardising the security of your assets and investments. I talk in more depth about structuring in chapter 21.

## Education

Emphasising the importance of education cannot be overstated. I began by addressing the greatest risk in life – the one you're unaware of – and through education, you can be sure you know of them all – at least in theory!

Most people I meet assume that because I'm a trader, I must be comfortable with taking big risks. But the opposite is true. Anyone who's been in markets for a long time will understand that risk management is the key to consistent growth.

## 5-POINT ACTION PLAN

1. Educate yourself and understand the different types of risks. Gaining knowledge about these risks will help you make informed decisions and better protect your capital.

2. Ensure that your investments match your financial objectives and the time horizon for achieving them. Be cautious with fixed-term and capital-guaranteed products.

3. To mitigate the impact of unforeseen events and market fluctuations, diversify your investments across various asset classes, sectors and geographic regions.

4. Use stop-loss orders as a part of your investment strategy to minimise potential losses on trades in the stock market.

5. Consult with a professional who specialises in asset protection and structuring to ensure your hard work and investments are safeguarded.

## ONLINE RESOURCES

Check out the online Success Portal at wealthplaybook.com for more on risk and reward.

# Chapter 11

# INVESTING IN EDUCATION

Be humble, or be prepared to be humbled.

Dennis Hogan

If you're like me and have never been taught to play a musical instrument, it's likely that sheet music will appear as a jumbled mess of lines and symbols. If someone were to give you the notes for Beethoven's Fifth Symphony and asked you to play it on the piano, you wouldn't even bother trying. Yet someone who has been taught can take the same symbols, lines and strange marks and turn them into beautiful music.

But, somewhat strangely, people don't seem to have the same resistance to trading as they do to playing music. Many people decide to jump in and try trading stocks without being able to read a chart! I have seen countless examples of people throwing tens of thousands of dollars into a trading account, vowing to 'learn as they go'.

Unfortunately, this rarely ends well. Until you know what all of the lines and markers represent, you won't be equipped to make the right decisions.

People who dive headfirst into investing may well see some initial short-term gains but, in the long run, they are likely to lose money. And most of the time, they won't even understand where they went wrong.

In order to come out on top in any game, you need to have a thorough understanding of the rules. Just as you wouldn't anticipate winning a game of chess without learning the necessary moves and strategies, you can't expect financial success without educating yourself on the fundamentals first.

## WHAT DO YOU NEED TO LEARN?

In an era of free information, it's easy to believe we know more than we actually do. But, as they say, 'you don't know what you don't know'. Once you begin your journey of financial education, you might be amazed at how much you have yet to learn!

Now, you can be confident that once you've read this book, you will have a much stronger knowledge base than the majority of the population. The lessons I provide in these pages give you an excellent understanding of what it takes to be financially successful. However, investment education is not a one-size-fits-all solution.

For example, if you're interested in investing in real estate, you may need to do a deep dive into cross-collateralisation, property development, financing, renovations or urban zoning. If you're interested in trading stocks, you may need to learn the intricacies of technical analysis, futures trading and risk-management strategies.

Knowledge gaps will also vary from person to person. It might be that you've been trading individual stocks for a decade, but know nothing about exchange-traded funds. It's crucial to assess your own shortcomings and seek out education that directly addresses them.

The following figure provides some ideas on the factors that might influence your financial literacy, and possible outcomes from improving it.

While it's tempting to try to learn everything at once, you should prioritise your learning and focus on the most essential knowledge first. This will help you avoid feeling overwhelmed and ensure that you're building a strong foundation for your financial success.

## Understanding Financial Literacy

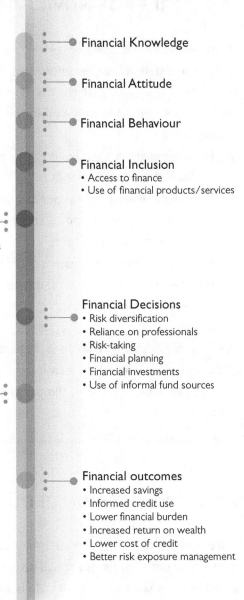

Financial Knowledge

Financial Attitude

Financial Behaviour

Financial Inclusion
- Access to finance
- Use of financial products / services

**Financial Well-being**
- Retirement planning
- Lesser impact of income shocks
- Wealth accumulation
- Smooth consumption
- Higher spending capacity
- Financial satisfaction
- Lower level of indebtness

**Financial Decisions**
- Risk diversification
- Reliance on professionals
- Risk-taking
- Financial planning
- Financial investments
- Use of informal fund sources

**Personal Background**
- Age
- Gender
- Marital status
- Race
- Religion
- Culture
- Parental influence
- Knowledge
  - numeracy
  - understanding of inflation
- Education
- Wealth
- Income
- Occupation
- Health
- Responsibilities
- Self-control
- Attitude towards
  - money
  - numbers
  - the future

**Financial outcomes**
- Increased savings
- Informed credit use
- Lower financial burden
- Increased return on wealth
- Lower cost of credit
- Better risk exposure management

## LESSON BLOCK: TIPS FOR NOVICE INVESTORS

Here are some tips novice investors are often not aware of until they've invested in financial education:

- Share prices usually fall the day after dividends are paid.
- You can use your superannuation to buy an investment property.
- Investing in art or rare coins can be a lucrative alternative to traditional stocks and bonds.
- Investing in foreign currencies can diversify your portfolio.
- You can use options trading strategies to hedge your portfolio against market volatility.
- Real estate investments trusts (REITs) can offer exposure to the real estate market, without owning physical property.
- The use of leverage in trading or investing can amplify gains and losses.

Of course, further education is required in all of these areas before putting an investment strategy in place. But these tips can give you an idea of some of the things you might not yet know about.

## CHOOSING THE RIGHT EDUCATOR

The hardest part about becoming financially literate can be working out which 'experts' to learn from. The internet is full of influencers promising to make you rich with their blogs, books, podcasts and courses. Some of the content is offered free, while some will cost you an upfront fee or ongoing periodical payments.

While it may be tempting to choose the information that costs you nothing, you need to be aware that the person or company offering you that material may well have an ulterior motive. Cynical as it may sound, if something is free, you are the commodity!

For example, a blogger who recommends investing in crypto-currencies may take a commission when you sign up for a cryptocurrency exchange through a link they've provided. There have also been cases of financial education websites offering free webinars as a way to gather your personal data and sell it to third-party companies for marketing purposes.

You should also do your homework before paying for any investment product or service. In today's online world, it is easy to fall victim to predatory operators who make you feel insecure about your knowledge and convince you to pay for something you don't need.

The best thing you can do is to find an education provider that has a track record of success. Look for reviews from other users and check if the provider has a good reputation in the industry. Consider if the provider has any conflicts of interest and if they are transparent about their affiliations.

You also want to be sure the content and advice is delivered in a way that you can understand and that ongoing support is provided throughout your investing journey. Usually, a one-off course won't be sufficient because your needs and the investing landscape will inevitably evolve over time.

Keep in mind also that no question should be too trivial. It's crucial to find an organisation that encourages inquiries and adopts a philosophy that welcomes all questions. Those clients who persistently ask questions and pursue knowledge are the ones who will ultimately succeed in their investment journey.

Consulting multiple sources and developing your own opinions based on diverse perspectives is also crucial. Embrace curiosity, ask questions and critically evaluate the information you come across.

## CASE STUDY: TORB STOLPE

Torbe Stolpe, an Adelaide grandfather, tried several types of investing throughout his life with varying levels of success.

He had developed some knowledge of the real estate market and what's known as 'naked options trading', but had been unable to achieve the results he was after.

In 2018, he decided it was time to learn new skills and attended a seminar by renowned author Robert Kiyosaki. At this seminar, he also saw a presentation by Australian Investment Education and later decided to sign up to our courses on Cashflow on Demand and Advanced Options Trading.

Torbe's dedication to learning paid off. Even during a market downturn in 2022, he was able to achieve a 30 per cent return on investment, equivalent to a profit of around $800 per week. He outperformed the S&P 500 index by more than 50 per cent and was named AIE's trader of the year!

This success allowed Torbe and his wife the flexibility to work less and travel more. He was well on the path to replacing his income and wished he had started sooner.

'I was 50 years old when I started and was financially free in five years,' Torbe said. 'Don't listen to friends and family who put doubt into you.'

Torbe succeeded by taking advantage of AIE's daily trade recommendations, helpful online community and personalised one-on-one support. He believes that partnering with a reliable and established financial education provider transformed his financial journey and, ultimately, his life.

As a testament to the impact of financial education, he now teaches financial skills to his children, viewing it as a meaningful legacy to leave behind.

## HOW MUCH SHOULD YOU PAY?

Education is an investment and, just like any other investment, you need to be prepared to spend money to see a return. But, at the same time, you don't want to pay for something that doesn't provide the value you were expecting.

The first thing to consider is what type of education you need. Do you just want some basic knowledge to get started? Or do you require a more in-depth understanding of a particular asset class? The amount you need to pay will depend on the level of education you require.

One way to determine the value of a program is to look at what you'll be learning. Are you learning skills that will directly translate into financial gain? Will you be learning how to identify and analyse potential investment opportunities? Or will you simply be learning basic concepts and terminology?

At first glance, the cost of financial education might seem high, but it is merely a small portion of the potential losses incurred due to poor decisions resulting from inadequate knowledge. In one of our podcast episodes, world boxing champion Dennis Hogan aptly remarked, 'One must either be humble, or be prepared to be humbled.'

Some people may believe they can learn independently or with a friend's assistance, but it's essential to acknowledge that financial education demands specialised skills and expertise that might not be immediately evident. By taking the time to recognise knowledge gaps and invest in tailored training, you can sidestep costly errors and establish processes and systems for lasting success. As your knowledge and skills grow, you can monitor your progress and identify any new knowledge gaps, and perhaps invest in more specialised training to keep achieving your goals.

# 5-POINT ACTION PLAN

1. Identify the areas where you lack knowledge or expertise and focus on addressing those gaps first. Prioritise your learning to build a strong foundation for your financial success.

2. Do thorough research to find a reputable and reliable education provider that meets your needs. Look for reviews from other users and check the provider's track record in the industry. Ensure the content is delivered in a way you understand and that ongoing support is provided throughout your investing journey.

3. Recognise that education is an investment in yourself, and the returns can be substantial if you choose the right program. Be prepared to spend money on quality education that will equip you with the skills and knowledge needed to succeed in the world of investing.

4. Embrace curiosity, ask questions, and critically evaluate the information you come across. Be open to new ideas, be humble, and absorb as much information as possible. Remember that no question is too trivial, and it's crucial to find an organisation that encourages inquiries and welcomes all questions.

5. Put your newfound knowledge and skills into practice and monitor your progress as you continue on your investment journey. Be prepared to adjust your strategies and continue learning as the investing landscape evolves over time. The more you learn and apply, the better equipped you will be to achieve your financial goals.

## ONLINE RESOURCES

Investing in Education is essential for staying ahead of the game, whether that be specialised or of a more general nature. Check out the free training session for mapping out your learning journey at wealthplaybook.com.au.

# Part III

# THE INVESTMENT UNIVERSE

# Chapter 12

# DUE DILIGENCE

Measure twice, cut once.

Common carpentry advice (also Dennis Baxter, my dad)

You can be forgiven for wanting to dive headfirst into your first major investment. The allure of big gains and ongoing passive income can be strong. But while this book is all about taking action, a level of due diligence must first be completed to ensure you're not leaping headfirst into shallow waters!

Just like apprentice carpenters are taught to 'measure twice and cut once', you should double-check all known parameters before pressing the 'go' button on any investment. Losing money because you didn't take the time to do so is unforgivable!

As someone who values process and structure, I have a checklist I go through before allocating any funds, regardless of the investment type – whether it's real estate, stocks or even starting a business.

So, in this chapter, let's look at the 10 questions from my checklist you should ask yourself before proceeding with any investment.

## HAVE YOU GENUINELY CONSIDERED THE INVESTMENT YOU'RE ABOUT TO MAKE?

Okay, this is a very simple question to start, but it's important to establish your answer to this before proceeding down the checklist. Ask yourself why you're making the investment. Have you conducted thorough research to come up with the idea yourself? Or are you taking advice from a friend or colleague? If the latter, how knowledgeable and experienced is that friend or colleague?

The influence of peer pressure can be strong and usually leads to poor choices. During recent booms in the cryptocurrency market, people were hearing of friends who had made incredible 10,000 per cent gains. These people then jumped in expecting the same returns. Unfortunately, by that point the hype was peaking and before long the only way was down.

Make sure you're investing for the right reasons. Fear of missing out (referred to as 'FOMO') is definitely not one of them! Take the time to determine what's suitable for your unique situation. Otherwise, you may end up feeling frustrated and eventually abandon your investment journey.

## DO YOU HAVE ENOUGH CAPITAL AVAILABLE TO INVEST?

Having a lump sum ready to invest is one thing, but do you also have enough to cover any ongoing costs associated with your investment?

Buying a rental property, for example, will likely require more than just your initial deposit. You also need to consider stamp duty and conveyancing fees as part of the purchase, as well as ongoing costs – which are sometimes cruelly unexpected.

Sure, rental income can help cover your interest payments and servicing costs, but you may have periods without tenants. And if the air conditioning system blows up, you could suddenly be thousands of dollars out of pocket.

Going into an investment with a significant savings buffer will help you sleep better and will ensure you're not forced to sell up if you incur unforeseen bills.

## WILL YOU BE MAKING REGULAR CONTRIBUTIONS TO YOUR INVESTMENT?

Increasing your investments beyond your initial lump sum can be a smart approach, especially when investing in the stock market. By consistently contributing additional funds to your portfolio, you can take advantage of what's known as 'dollar-cost averaging'.

Dollar-cost averaging is a technique where an investor manages the impact of market volatility by making periodic purchases of a target asset. This spreads the investment over time, mitigating the effects of market fluctuations on the overall cost basis.

For instance, you might invest an initial $20,000 in stocks and then commit to investing an additional $1000 each month. This means you'll invest at varying market prices – some months at higher prices, and other months at lower prices. The theory is that over time, you will balance out the purchase price of your investments and reduce the impact of market timing on your overall returns.

Ultimately, finding the right mix between your initial investment and regular contributions will help you create a more stable and diversified investment strategy.

## ARE YOU AN ACTIVE OR PASSIVE INVESTOR?

Choosing whether to pursue an active or passive investment strategy will be one of the most important decisions you make. And this decision will then have flow-on effects when considering individual investment options.

Active investments can be highly lucrative but will require a lot of your time and energy. You will need to regularly manage your portfolio, and make frequent buy and sell decisions based on market research, analysis and personal judgements.

Passive investing, on the other hand, focuses on long-term growth by holding onto investments and minimising the number of trades made. The input from you is usually minimal.

Deciding what is right for you will depend on a number of factors. Do you have the time, knowledge and expertise to try to outperform the market with an active investment strategy, such as share trading individual stocks? Or would you prefer to match the market's performance by investing in diversified index funds or exchange-traded funds (ETFs) that track specific market indices?

Carefully weighing the pros and cons of both approaches, while also considering your individual circumstances, will help you determine the optimal strategy to achieve your financial goals. You can then apply this strategy to individual investment options.

## WHAT IS YOUR INVESTMENT TIME FRAME?

Successful Australian entrepreneur Mark Bouris often speaks about the importance of having an exit strategy. And he says that exit strategy should be formulated before any commitments are made. This involves considering your desired outcome, identifying potential exit options and setting an investment time frame.

If you're buying shares, when do you plan to cash out? Are you looking to fund your retirement? Or are you investing for your child's university education? Each of those scenarios and their time frames will require different strategies to ensure your investment matures at the right time.

Depending on your personality type, it may well be that you never want to sell your investment and instead want to continue enjoying the returns. I have a friend who has never sold an asset in his life – and it works for him. But it doesn't for everyone.

Another factor to consider that relates to time frame is the liquidity of your investments and how easily you can access the funds when required. Different asset types offer varying levels of liquidity, with shares typically being more liquid than properties.

## WHAT ARE YOUR SKILLS AND VALUES?

Planning to invest in an industry or sector you know nothing about is a very clear red flag. Where possible, always align your investment strategy with your skills, values and interests. Being passionate about a specific area or industry can lead to a deeper understanding of its potential.

For example, when it comes to property investments, being able to identify up-and-coming neighbourhoods is a skill that will prove lucrative. Similarly, if you have the skills to carry out renovations, such as repainting or installing new flooring, you can enhance the property's value and potential returns.

More substantial improvements, such as fitting a new kitchen, can also make a significant difference. This so-called sweat equity can be a valuable asset if you possess the skills, determination and commitment to undertake such projects. But if you're lacking those attributes, perhaps steer clear!

As for investing in the stock market, you should consider whether you have the skills and commitment to maximise your chances of success. Later in the book I discuss how knowledge of strategies such as Cashflow on Demand or the use of covered calls can boost returns and minimise risk. You can educate yourself on specific skill shortages (as covered in the previous chapter and the next section), but also ask yourself whether these types of strategies align with your overall skills, values and behaviours.

## CAN YOU EDUCATE YOURSELF ABOUT THE INVESTMENT?

If you don't have the relevant skills required for your desired investment, work out how you will fill those knowledge gaps. If, for example, you're about to invest a million dollars in an investment property, spending an extra few thousand on a real estate investment course is a sound idea.

Unfortunately, some people undervalue the importance of education and skills development. This lack of foresight can lead to costly mistakes that require the expertise of legal or financial professionals to rectify.

By investing in your education and taking the time to upskill, you can avoid these pitfalls and ensure you're adequately prepared. In the long run, the knowledge you gain will prove invaluable, saving you time, money and potential headaches.

## DO YOU UNDERSTAND THE ECONOMIC FACTORS THAT COULD IMPACT YOUR INVESTMENT?

Understanding how your investment is likely to perform under various economic conditions is an essential skill. You'll often see disclaimers on investment products that say 'past performance is not an indicator of future performance', but most of the time, it is!

In chapter 10, I mention that during times of high inflation, real estate and gold traditionally perform well, while certain stocks do not. During times of global unrest, for example, companies in the utilities and defence sectors generally increase in value.

If you feel you don't have sufficient understanding of how the broader economy works, it might be beneficial to outsource some of this heavy lifting to professionals. By asking them to share their insights on the current state of the economy and which asset classes or sectors they expect to perform best, you can make them truly earn their fees.

This approach not only helps you get valuable information but also ensures that you're taking control of your investment decisions. Remember, you don't need to be the smartest person in the room. Instead, focus on asking smart questions and utilising the expertise of others to your advantage.

## WHAT RISKS ARE ASSOCIATED WITH THE INVESTMENT?

Understanding the potential risks associated with different investments is crucial, and this is where due diligence really comes into play. Consider the best- and worst-case scenarios, the track record of the investment, and any audited data or statistics that may be available.

Examine the regulatory environment and seek advice from clients who have used similar services. Understand the potential downside of investments and the factors that could negatively impact them.

For example, while property investments might seem safe due to the constant need for housing, they can be affected by various factors, such as market swings and changes in interest rates. You must be prepared for unforeseen circumstances and have a contingency plan in place.

## WHAT IS YOUR PERSONAL RISK PROFILE?

Everyone's attitude to risk is different, and understanding your risk profile is essential for making sound investment decisions.

Many factors determine your risk profile, including your genetic make-up! Some of us are more disposed to taking on risk than others, and the chances are if your parents and siblings are comfortable with financial risks, you probably will be too. You can take various online questionnaires to help you understand where you are on the scale.

Other things to consider when it comes to risk include your age and current situation. Generally, the younger you are, the more risk you'll be prepared to take on. This is because if the market swings downwards, you will have time to wait for it to bounce back! On the other side of the coin, someone approaching retirement will usually have a low risk profile because their investing time frame is much shorter.

What's most important is not to be influenced by the attitudes of others, because doing so can lead to decisions that aren't true to your nature, resulting in anxiety and restless nights. Don't be swayed by a false sense of bravado, and instead invest according to your true risk tolerance.

When making investment decisions with a partner, involve them in the process even if they prefer to be hands-off. Catering to different attitudes between partners can lead to a more balanced and suitable approach for the couple as a whole.

## WHAT'S NEXT?

After reflecting on the 10 questions presented in this chapter, you'll be equipped to either move forward with your investment or consider exploring other opportunities.

As you gain experience and expertise in your chosen asset class, you'll naturally encounter more in-depth questions and risk assessments. Embrace professional guidance and education to understand and mitigate these risks effectively. Establish your goals and game plan, and approach your investment journey with a sequential and proactive mindset.

## 5-POINT ACTION PLAN

1. Refer back to this chapter each time you are about to proceed with any investment. Take the time to answer the 10 fundamental questions to ensure the investment is right for you.
2. Block out external noise from friends, family and work colleagues to ensure you're acting on your own research and independently sought advice.
3. Decide whether you wish to be an active or passive investor based on your available time, knowledge and expertise.
4. Consider your skills, values and interests and whether you need education to fill any knowledge gaps.
5. Assess your risk profile by taking into account factors such as your age, current situation and personality.

## ONLINE RESOURCES

Due diligence is always worth doing before, not after the fact! At wealthplaybook.com.au we have prepared a free due diligence tutorial to help you make the most informed decisions when it comes to your investing.

# Chapter 13

# MANAGED INVESTMENTS

Are managed funds giving you a false sense of security?

Andrew Baxter

For decades, managed investments, also referred to as mutual funds, managed funds or investment funds, have stood as a pillar in the investment landscape. They've offered a platform for everyday people – the so-called mum and dad investors – to entrust their money to professionals, whose job is to use their knowledge to grow the capital.

On the surface, the concept seems quite appealing. The experts offer investors a straightforward, passive way to build their wealth and, in return, receive a fee for their services. Indeed, when a fund performs well, it's a win for both parties.

However, the reality is that more often than not, it's exclusively the fund managers who reap the benefits. Research has shown the majority of actively managed funds fail to outperform passive index funds, meaning a lot of investors are essentially paying more in fees, but are not seeing a genuine benefit from this.

In this chapter, I explain how managed investments work, why many people embrace them, and why others are beginning to look elsewhere.

# THE MECHANICS OF MANAGED INVESTMENTS

The role of fund managers is to pool money from multiple investors and deploy the collective capital into a diversified portfolio of assets. These assets can include a mix of equities, bonds, commodities, real estate, and even more specialised investments such as private equity or hedge funds.

Each investor in a managed fund owns units or shares, which represent a portion of the holdings of the fund. The value of these units fluctuates based on the performance of the underlying assets in the fund's portfolio. Profits from the fund can be distributed to investors in the form of dividends or capital gains, or they can be reinvested back into the fund to purchase more units.

At the helm of each managed fund is the fund manager. Their role involves extensive research and analysis to make informed decisions about where to allocate the fund's assets. They aim to generate a return for investors, either by achieving growth in the value of the investments (capital growth) or by earning income from the investments (such as dividends or interest), or a combination of both.

Investors can typically buy into or sell out of managed funds at the fund's net asset value (NAV) per share, which is usually calculated daily based on the total value of the fund's assets minus any liabilities, divided by the number of shares outstanding.

## The benefits

Managed funds have been popular among a wide range of investors for a long period of time for many reasons. The benefits of managed funds include:

- *Professional management:* A fund manager who has the knowledge, experience and resources to deliver outperformance can be invaluable. While hard to find, they provide peace of mind and can save you significant time and effort compared to managing your own investments.

- *Diversification:* Managed investments can allow individual investors, who might not have the significant capital required to build a diverse portfolio individually, to gain exposure to a broad range of assets. This means you can spread risk by ensuring your portfolio doesn't hinge on a single or small group of investments.

- *Accessibility:* Managed funds offer a relatively low entry point for investment, making them accessible to the average investor. Through a managed fund, it's possible to hold positions in everything from US 20-year treasuries to UK gilts and German bonds, which could otherwise be out of reach.

- *Liquidity:* Most managed investments can be easily bought or sold on any business day, providing flexibility and easy access to your money. This feature is particularly beneficial for investors who want the ability to quickly react to changing personal circumstances or market conditions.

- *Range of investment options:* Managed funds come in a wide variety of types, with each designed to cater to different investment goals, risk tolerances and time horizons. Whether you're looking for income, growth, capital preservation, or a combination, there's likely a managed fund marketed to suit your needs.

- *Convenience:* Managed funds can make the investment process easier for investors. At the end of the tax year, they provide investors with a consolidated statement that simplifies the tracking of their investments. They also handle other administrative work, including record-keeping and reinvesting dividends or distributions. This convenience allows investors to focus on their broader financial goals rather than the day-to-day management of their portfolio.

- *Transparency:* An investment portfolio within a managed fund is typically valued on a daily basis, allowing investors to easily track its performance each day. This level of transparency allows investors to make timely decisions if necessary.

- *Regular income streams:* Certain types of managed funds, such as bond or income funds, can provide investors with regular income streams through dividends or interest payments. This can be an attractive feature for those seeking a steady income, such as retirees.

## The drawbacks

Unfortunately, a managed fund is rarely the perfect investment solution. Some of the most common pitfalls include:

- *High costs:* Managed funds usually come with annual fees of between 0.5 and 2.5 per cent of your total funds under management. While they may seem relatively insignificant at first glance, they can significantly reduce your investment's growth potential. Unlike a hedge fund, where managers usually take a percentage of profits, most managed funds collect their flat fee regardless of performance.

- *Underperformance:* I have already touched on the elephant in the room, but now I'm going to be more specific. Multiple studies by SPIVA, a well-regarded comparison and ratings facility, have shown that around 80 per cent of Australian equity general funds underperform the S&P/ASX 200, Australia's leading share market index. (See the table at the end of this bulleted list; for the latest report in this area, just search for 'SPIVA Australia Scorecard' online.) This shows that despite the promise of fund managers' expertise and specialised knowledge in certain sectors, the majority struggle to outperform basic benchmarks.

- *Potential for overweighting:* Investors should also be aware of the potential for overweighting in managed funds. Often, they will allocate a significant portion of the portfolio to domestic equities, deeming them less risky due to familiarity and the absence of exchange rate risk. However, this approach may not be the most rational when considering the global economy. For example, while Australia accounts for only 1.8 per cent of the global economy, it's common for Australian funds to allocate 40 per cent of investments to it. On the other hand, the United States, constituting over 50 per cent of the global economy, might only receive a 10 to 15 per cent allocation.

- *Slow reaction times:* Many funds have long gaps between portfolio reviews, which makes it difficult for them to react swiftly to market shifts and any changes in inflation. Much like an oil tanker, they often require substantial time and distance to change course. This sluggish manoeuvrability can leave them trailing behind in rapidly evolving economic climates, often missing opportunities or failing to mitigate risks in a timely manner.

- *Lock-in periods:* Some managed funds come with lock-in periods during which investors are not allowed to withdraw their investment. The constraint of a lock-in period may not align with your financial needs, particularly if you require liquidity or access to your funds in the short term. Further, if the fund's performance isn't up to par or if better investment opportunities are available elsewhere, you're unable to reallocate your capital.

- *Conflicts of interest:* Lastly, it's important to note potential conflicts of interest within the managed funds industry. Financial advisors, especially those affiliated with 'dealer groups' (that is, a group that employs large numbers of financial planners, offering them training, licensing and support services), often operate with approved product lists, which limit the range of funds they can recommend to clients. These lists tend to favour funds managed by the dealer group, which may not always provide the best performance.

**Percentage of Australian managed funds that have underperformed the Index**

| Fund Category | Comparison Index | 1-Year (%) | 3-Year (%) | 5-Year (%) | 10-Year (%) | 15-Year (%) |
|---|---|---|---|---|---|---|
| Australian Equity General | S&P/ASX 200 | 57.56 | 65.32 | 81.18 | 78.22 | 83.57 |
| International Equity General | S&P Developed Ex-Australia LargeMidCap | 56.29 | 80.78 | 86.25 | 95.00 | 94.30 |

Source: S&P Dow Jones Indices LLC, Morningstar. Data for periods ending Dec. 30, 2022. Outperformance is based on equal-weighted fund counts. Index performance based on total return. Past performance is no guarantee of future results. Table is provided for illustrative purposes.

S&P® and S&P 500® are registered trademarks of Standard & Poor's Financial Services LLC, and Dow Jones® is a registered trademark of Dow Jones Trademark Holdings LLC. © 2023 S&P Dow Jones Indices LLC, its affiliates and/or its licensors. All rights reserved.

## The verdict

While managed funds may have been the norm in the past, it's clear that times are changing. Unless you happen to have the knack of picking that one of the one in five fund managers who's going to outperform the market, you're signing up to pay a fee for a subpar result.

In my opinion, direct share investments or exchange-traded funds (ETFs) can offer much better long-term value. In the following two chapters, we will explore those alternatives and look at how you can use them to build significant lasting wealth.

## 5-POINT ACTION PLAN

1. Equip yourself with a good understanding of how managed funds work, their benefits, and their drawbacks.

2. Thoroughly understand the fee structures of any fund you consider investing in. Some funds may have high expense ratios that can eat into your returns, while others may have additional costs such as sales loads or redemption fees.

3. Decide whether managed funds are right for you. If you're uncomfortable with the potential downsides, it might be time to explore other avenues.

4. Consider professional advice. While potential conflicts of interest exist with some financial advisors, an independent and reliable advisor can provide valuable insights and guidance. Ensure they are independent and not tied to a particular product list.

5. Research alternatives. ETFs can be a compelling alternative to managed funds because of their cost-effectiveness, flexibility and ability to track market indices. By investing in an ETF that tracks a market index, you are statistically likely to outperform 80 per cent of managed funds.

## ONLINE RESOURCES

Understanding how managed funds are rated will assist you in picking those that best suit your needs. We have prepared a tutorial for you at wealthplaybook.com.au that will assist you in identifying whether managed funds may be suitable for you and which ones would be more appropriate.

# Chapter 14

# DIRECT SHARE INVESTMENTS

Buy wisely, hold patiently, sell strategically.

Andrew Baxter

I'll begin this chapter with some more words of wisdom from my father. From the moment I started working, he would say, 'Don't put your money in the bank; put your money into bank shares.'

His theory was that receiving a slice of the vast profits generated by major UK institutions such as Lloyds Bank or Barclays would be more beneficial than depending on the modest interest offered by their savings accounts.

History has shown Dad's advice to be sound. If you deposited $100,000 in a savings account offering a 2 per cent interest rate in 2003, your balance would have grown to $148,595 by 2023. However, if instead you used that $100,000 to buy shares in American banking powerhouse JP Morgan, your portfolio would have swelled to an eye-watering $762,602 over the same 20-year period.

For those who remained faithful to traditional bank interest over that time, the difference would be enough to induce tears of regret. But it's important to remember that investing is always easy in hindsight and shares never come without their own set of risks. While

JP Morgan has sustained its success over decades, you could just as easily have invested in a firm like Lehman Brothers, which famously declared bankruptcy in 2008.

The key to direct share investing is not only knowing which stocks to buy, but also knowing when to hold them and when to sell them. And the only way to get that right on a consistent basis is by equipping yourself with knowledge and developing a bulletproof strategy.

Without doubt, buying shares can be a great way to begin your investing journey. Potential profits aside, you will learn a lot simply by going through the process of establishing a stockbroking account, funding the account and then making informed decisions on the companies in which you'd like to invest.

In this chapter, we'll dive into the fundamentals to help you begin your journey.

## WHAT IS DIRECT SHARE INVESTING?

Let's begin with the basics. Direct share investing, or individual stock investing, involves buying shares in a company straight from a stock exchange. This approach is distinctly different from investing in managed funds, where your investment is combined with those of other investors and is overseen by a professional fund manager. In the realm of direct share investing, you maintain full control and are solely responsible for making your investment decisions.

As a shareholder, you become a part-owner of the company, no matter how small your share, and you may be entitled to a portion of the company's profits in the form of dividends. The value of your investment will rise or fall with the performance of the company.

If the company performs well and its profits increase, the value of your shares may rise. However, if the company faces financial difficulties or the overall market declines, the value of your shares may fall. That's why direct share investing carries a level of risk and requires careful research and consideration.

# VALUATION DIFFERENCES

The valuation of a company is determined by various factors, including its earnings, growth potential, assets and market conditions. The decision whether to buy high valuation stocks (referred to as 'blue-chip stocks') or low valuation stocks (referred to as 'penny stocks') will depend on your risk appetite and time horizon.

## Blue-chip stocks

Blue-chip stocks are usually the titans of industry – the largest and most recognised companies within any given stock market. These firms often hold a prominent place within the top 50 list of any stock exchange.

In Australia, this list would typically include the big four banks, mining giants such as BHP and Rio Tinto, retail behemoths Woolworths and Coles, and healthcare leader CSL. If we were to shift our gaze to the US market, blue chip companies include household names such as Apple, Google, Microsoft, JP Morgan and American Airlines.

These companies aren't just names on an index or ticker tape – they're integral parts of our daily lives. Their high profiles are backed by substantial, long-standing businesses. They are not fledglings, and they're unlikely to provide the quick short-term returns that some fledglings can (if you pick the right one). But they are time-tested enterprises that have demonstrated a consistent ability to generate profits and deliver value to their shareholders.

As a starting point in your investment journey, blue-chip stocks can provide a degree of stability and reliability.

## 'Penny' stocks

On the opposite end of the spectrum from the stalwart blue-chip stocks, we find what are known as 'penny stocks', or more colloquially 'penny dreadfuls'. It's important to note that these stocks don't necessarily sell for just a few pennies; however, they do have lower valuations than their blue-chip counterparts.

Penny stocks often represent smaller, emerging companies, perhaps venturing into the mining sector or launching a novel technology. Because their business concepts are often unproven and their futures uncertain, these stocks tend to be much more volatile and speculative. They usually come with higher risk – and the potential for higher reward.

New businesses often start their public life as penny stocks, essentially asking the market, 'What do you think of our new concept?' As they prove their viability and earn the trust of investors, these companies can gradually ascend the ranks. Some might even attain the coveted status of a blue-chip stock!

Investing in penny stocks can be a riskier venture, but it also offers the opportunity to be part of a company's growth story right from the start.

## DOMESTIC VERSUS INTERNATIONAL SHARES

When buying shares, an important consideration is whether to choose domestic or international companies. By 'domestic', I mean stocks listed on your home country's exchange, while 'international' encompasses stocks listed on major global exchanges worldwide.

When you're starting out, domestic stocks can be the way to go because the businesses are usually familiar and brokerage platforms generally cater primarily to the local market they operate in, making it more straightforward for beginners.

However, as mentioned in the previous chapter, the Australian economy represents merely 1.8 per cent of the global economy, and concentrating all investment within this relatively small segment might mean missing out on lucrative global opportunities – or, worse, being over exposed to risk.

## MAKING PROFITS

It goes without saying that the primary purpose of buying shares is to make money, so now let's look at the two ways to profit from direct share investing.

### Capital gains

Perhaps the most obvious way shares can make you profits is by increasing in value! The strategy here is simple: buy low and sell high.

This approach is typically associated with 'growth stocks', many of which are penny stocks. Afterpay, a 'buy now, pay later' platform, is an Australian success story where early investors saw significant returns. In 2017, you could have purchased Afterpay shares for around $5 each, and in 2021 you could have sold them for around $150 – that's a whopping 2900 per cent return on your initial investment.

Capital gains investing is often suitable for risk-tolerant investors seeking aggressive growth. While this strategy carries the potential for high returns due to price appreciation, it also carries inherent volatility, which can lead to significant losses.

### Dividends

The more passive way to profit from shares is through dividends, which many companies pay out to their shareholders as a share of their profit. These payments are usually made annually, quarterly or monthly, depending on the company's policy.

Dividends hold particular appeal in Australia because of its unique franking credit system. Fully franked dividends indicate that the corporation has already paid tax on that profit. As a result, you're only liable for additional tax if your personal tax rate exceeds the corporate tax rate. If your tax rate is lower, you become eligible for a tax credit.

It's important to note that dividend stocks can also grow in value, allowing you to also make capital gains. Many investors have had success by using their dividends to buy additional company shares, accelerating the compounding of wealth over time.

## BUYING CRITERIA

Before rushing out to buy shares, it's important to do your homework. It's alarming how many people set aside large amounts of money and decide to 'give it a go' and learn along the way. More often than not, these investors lose money.

My advice is to ask yourself the following questions before throwing your money behind any company.

### Does the company offer something useful?

A company should provide a product or service that is in demand or essential. Utilities companies, for example, offer services that people can't do without, making them reliable investments, particularly during uncertain economic times.

### Is the company future-proof?

It's crucial that companies that are forward-thinking and continually adapting to economic and social trends. These companies evolve to better position themselves in the market.

Amazon serves as a prime example, having transformed from an online bookstore into a multifaceted e-commerce giant. Movie rental company Blockbuster, on the other hand, failed to see the future of online streaming services and passed on the opportunity to acquire Netflix for a mere $70 million. Today, Netflix is valued in the hundreds of billions, while Blockbuster is now extinct.

Investing in companies that meet today's needs while also being geared towards the demands of tomorrow is crucial.

## Is the company profitable?

Before buying a company's shares, review its financial statements and take note of its revenue streams, expenses and net income. Consistent positive net income indicates that the company is generating profits, which is a positive sign. It's also beneficial to assess the company's profit margins to understand how efficiently it operates and whether it can sustain profitability over the long term.

## Is the company's stock price chart healthy?

Examining a company's stock price chart will help to determine the optimal time to buy shares. This process is called 'technical analysis' and doesn't need to be as complicated as it sounds. It's important to remember, however, that news and fundamentals can cause price movements that even the best chart readers can't predict.

## Is the company's stock price stable?

If you're looking for a stable stock, make sure its price hasn't historically been volatile, and vice-versa! Not all stocks have the same level of volatility, with some being more 'spicy' and prone to larger price fluctuations, while others are considered more 'mild' with more stable price movements.

With the right education, you can evaluate the stability of a company's stock price by incorporating quantitative analysis (quants), which uses mathematical models and statistical techniques to analyse data.

## Is your portfolio adequately diversified?

You may have found a great stock, but how does it fit into your broader portfolio? If you're investing in a bank, but already own three other bank stocks it's possible that you're placing too many eggs in one basket and need to sell one or two.

However, it's also important not to 'overdiversify', particularly if you have a strong conviction about a specific sector or company.

## Is 'FOMO' driving your decision?

Avoid making investment decisions solely based on the fear of missing out (FOMO). FOMO-driven investments – influenced by workplace chatter or neighbourhood gossip, for example – are typically not strong long-term prospects. Controlling FOMO is a key aspect of successful investing.

## WHERE TO BUY SHARES

These days many online platforms offer access to shares, but be careful about where you're depositing your money because the internet is full of dubious operators. If you're in Australia, ensure the platform carries an Australian financial services (AFS) licence and try to avoid sending money offshore whenever possible, because it can compromise your consumer protection rights.

If you want access to overseas shares, this is still possible via Australian brokers. Our platform, for example, allows you to invest in 78 markets worldwide, all from an Australian-based account using Australian dollars. Our team also assists with tasks such as filling out forms to ensure you're only obliged to pay tax in Australia and not overseas.

When choosing a platform, consider the competitiveness of the brokerage fees but don't get caught in the trap of going with what appears to be the cheapest option. There are always trade-offs.

Reliable data and quality customer support are critically important. In times of need, being able to talk to a human rather than a chatbot can save you significant stress and potentially even financial loss. It's often worth paying a little extra for that level of service.

## GET STARTED!

As you venture into investing, remember: the best time to start was yesterday. Educate yourself about the stock market, come up with a rock-solid strategy and find your niche. If you're looking for safe, long-term bets, look at blue-chip stocks, but if you're happy to take on some risk, don't be afraid to add some penny stocks to your portfolio.

I remember the fear I had to overcome, in my youth in Swindon, to take my hard-earned money and expose it to the market's risks. It's a significant step that requires immense courage, but with the right process it will pay off.

My parting advice, however, is that you shouldn't just blindly hold stocks for the long term. Just like maintaining a garden, a portfolio needs regular attention – pruning and weeding – to keep it healthy and growing.

---

### 5-POINT ACTION PLAN

1. Before investing in shares, it's crucial to gain knowledge about stock market dynamics and individual companies. Understand what direct share investing entails, the risks involved and the benefits it could bring. Do your homework on companies you're considering investing in: explore their business model, profitability, adaptability and stock price history.

2. Identify your risk appetite and goals. Are you an aggressive growth investor willing to take on more risk with potential high returns, or are you more conservative, preferring stable stocks with regular dividends?

3. Create a balanced and diversified portfolio. This includes investing in a mix of blue-chip and penny stocks, domestic and international shares. This strategy could help you manage risk and maximise your potential returns.

**4.** Select a trading platform that's reliable and has a strong reputation. Consider factors such as brokerage fees, the quality of customer support and the range of markets accessible through the platform.

**5.** Regularly monitor your portfolio and the performance of individual stocks. Be ready to adjust your portfolio based on changing market conditions, company performance, and shifts in your financial goals or risk appetite. Remember, direct share investing isn't a 'set it and forget it' endeavour.

## ONLINE RESOURCES

How to choose which shares to buy and when is a high level skill, requiring specialised training. We have prepared a free How To Invest in Shares workshop for you to learn more on this critical subject at wealthplaybook.com.au.

# Chapter 15

# EXCHANGE-TRADED FUNDS

Exchange-traded funds give you a world of
possibilities in a single trade.

Andrew Baxter

Exchange-traded funds, more commonly referred to as ETFs, didn't
exist when I began my investing career, but I wish they had. Despite
what many investors think, they can be incredible wealth-building
vehicles, regardless of whether you're a beginner or a seasoned
professional.

It's a regret of mine that I didn't embrace ETFs sooner. The myth
that they're boring and only offer very slow results simply isn't true.
In fact, once you know what you're doing, they can be one of the
most sophisticated investment tools in the market – and can behave
in a very spicy and volatile way!

I have personally grown to love ETFs, and I also think they could
be a game changer for you. In this chapter, I'll explain why.

## WHAT IS AN ETF?

An ETF pools together investors' money to purchase a diversified portfolio of assets, such as stocks, bonds and commodities. Generally, they function in a manner similar to managed funds, but have several unique characteristics.

Unlike managed funds, ETFs are tradeable on stock exchanges, just like any standard stock. The value of an ETF's shares will change throughout the trading day as they're bought and sold on the market. They also typically have lower fees than managed funds and offer high liquidity.

Essentially, ETFs allow investors to diversify their portfolios without needing to purchase all the individual assets within the fund.

If you think of the stock market as a supermarket filled with thousands of different items, then an ETF is like a pre-filled shopping cart. You can pick a cart that has only the things you are interested in, or indeed a little bit of everything. Better yet, it comes packaged together in a single product, allowing for a broad exposure to multiple companies, industries or even entire economies.

## EVOLUTION OF ETFS

The first ETF was introduced in 1993 and is known as the SPDR (Standard & Poor's Depositary Receipts) S&P 500 ETF. Often referred to by its ticker symbol 'SPY', the ETF was designed to track the performance of the S&P 500 index, one of the most widely followed stock market indices in the world.

The creation of the ETF marked a significant milestone in the investment industry, and its success paved the way for the growth and popularity of ETFs worldwide. Investors quickly began to appreciate them for providing the diversification benefits of managed funds with the tradeability and transparency of individual stocks.

Today, SPY remains one of the most heavily traded and widely recognised ETFs globally, with billions of dollars in assets under management. However, ETF offerings have also expanded to cover various other asset classes and investment strategies.

Passive ETFs, which aim to replicate the performance of an index, continue to dominate the market. However, more actively managed ETFs have gained popularity, allowing skilled fund managers to actively select and manage the underlying assets based on their expertise and investment strategies.

Advancements in technology and the rise of digital platforms have facilitated the growth of ETF investing, with online brokerages allowing them to be accessed and traded within minutes.

## BENEFITS OF ETFS

ETFs are particularly useful for novice investors because of their passive nature and proven track record of strong performance.

One notable advantage is their suitability for regular savings plans because of the relatively low transaction fees. If, for example, you've managed to save an extra $1000 and you want to track the market's performance, you can instantly gain an S&P 500 portfolio by investing in the SPY ETF.

As mentioned in chapter 13, a significant proportion of managed funds (approximately 80 per cent) fail to surpass market performance. That means ETFs that closely mirror market indexes not only come with lower fees but also usually offer better prospects than managed funds.

An additional benefit of ETFs lies in their transparency. The public typically has access to information on what an ETF holds, with at least the top 10 or 20 holdings being disclosed.

This is a stark contrast to managed funds, which often operate behind closed doors. As a former fund manager, I can attest to the fact that revealing positions in real time is never an option (it would be commercially sensitive, due in part to the large volume being traded with each position) – they were discussed only after the positions were closed.

The transparency of ETFs not only helps you make sound decisions but also allows investors to ensure the fund's holdings align with their social and moral values. Many, for example, wish to invest in companies that operate in the best interests of the environment. They can then choose an ETF that also invests based on these principles.

The table on the following page shows you the key features of ETFs and how they compare to those of managed funds.


## ETF PROVIDERS

While ETFs are often very passive investment vehicles, they still need to be managed by someone! This process primarily involves tracking and replicating the performance of a specific index or benchmark.

When considering which ETF provider to use, several factors come into play but my advice is to pick the biggest one! That's not to say that the biggest is best, but usually they do have better liquidity, transaction costs are generally lower and more advanced traders (like me) have more opportunities to use options to hedge against downside risk and enhance profits.

Some well-known and established ETF providers include Vanguard, BlackRock's iShares and SPDR by State Street Global Advisers. Vanguard is renowned for its low-cost index funds and ETFs, making it a popular choice for long-term, passive investors.

It's important to consider the specific investment objectives and preferences when selecting an ETF provider. Evaluate the provider's fund offerings to ensure they align with your investment goals. Also don't forget to consider the provider's customer service, educational resources and overall reputation within the industry.

## Exchange Traded Funds vs Managed Funds

|  | **ETFs** | **Managed funds (mutual funds)** |
|---|---|---|
| Structure | Traded on stock exchanges as shares | Bought and sold through the fund company at net asset value (NAV) |
| Trading | Intraday trading at market prices | Once per day at the fund's closing NAV |
| Transparency | Holdings disclosed | Holdings usually disclosed annually, quarterly or monthly |
| Expense ratios | Generally lower | Can be higher |
| Investment style | Can be passive or active management | Can be passive or active management |
| Minimum investment | Varies, can be low or no minimum | Varies, often higher minimum investment required |
| Flexibility | Can be traded throughout the trading day | Trades executed at the next NAV price |
| Capital gains tax | Typically more tax efficient | Capital gains triggered by individual redemptions |
| Sales load | Typically no sales load | May have sales load or transaction fees |
| Liquidity | High liquidity | Liquidity depends on redemption policy of the fund |
| Customisation | Limited ability to customise holdings | More flexibility to customise holdings |

## NICHE ETFS

These days, ETFs are available that offer very specialised invest-ment opportunities and strategies. Whether you're looking to hedge positions, seek leveraged exposure to the market or profit from a global news event or disaster, you can usually find a specific ETF to cater for your situation.

Some examples of these more niche ETFs include the following.

### Bond market ETFs

Bond market ETFs provide investors with a convenient and effi-cient way to gain exposure to the fixed income market. These ETFs typically track a specific bond index or segment of the bond market, offering diversification across various types of bonds, such as government bonds, corporate bonds or municipal bonds.

Bond market ETFs offer a cost-effective alternative to individ-ual bond investing, because they eliminate the need for direct bond purchases and provide access to a diversified portfolio of bonds in a single trade. They can be particularly useful for investors looking to profit in rising or falling interest rate environments.

### Inverse ETFs

Inverse ETFs offer investment opportunities for those anticipat-ing market declines. An ETF known as 'SH', for example, inversely tracks the S&P 500, meaning that as the market decreases, SH's value increases.

In Australia, an aptly named 'BEAR' ETF seeks to generate returns that are negatively correlated to the returns of the Austra-lian share market. (A 'bear' investor is one who believes a particular share or the broader market is headed downward and may attempt to profit from a decline in stock prices.)

## Geared ETFs

Geared or leveraged ETFs offer investors the opportunity to enhance exposure and potentially generate higher returns in a short period. For example, a geared ETF tracking the S&P 500 may seek to provide twice the daily return of the index.

It's important to note that these ETFs come with increased risks. They may not accurately reflect the long-term performance of the underlying index and can deviate significantly from expected returns over longer holding periods.

Geared ETFs are intended for short-term trading and active management strategies. Holding them for an extended period can lead to negative returns, especially in volatile markets. Therefore, they are best suited for experienced traders who understand the complexities of leverage, have a thorough risk management strategy, and actively monitor market conditions.

## Special situations ETFs

Special situations ETFs offer investors the opportunity to target niche areas of the market or take advantage of specific market dynamics.

For example, an ETF focused on renewable energy may invest in companies involved in solar, wind or hydroelectric power. Similarly, following the pandemic, an ETF focusing on pet care services performed well because people suddenly needed vets, groomers and walkers for the pets they'd purchased to keep them company during lockdowns.

Some ETFs even specifically target the decline of brick-and-mortar retail stores because of the rise of e-commerce giants such as Amazon. Not surprisingly, those also performed well during and after the pandemic.

Special situations ETFs can also be designed to capture opportunities arising from specific market conditions or events. For instance, ETFs focused on volatility indices, such as the VIX, allow investors to profit from market volatility.

Investing in special situations ETFs requires careful consideration and understanding of the underlying market dynamics. You should assess your risk tolerance and conduct thorough research to ensure the ETF aligns with your skills, knowledge and experience.

## GETTING STARTED WITH ETFS

Starting an investment journey with ETFs is an effective and straightforward choice, especially if you have idle cash.

I advocate the use of a 'solar system' investment model, where ETFs that track large market indices, such as the S&P 500, make up your largest holding (the sun), smaller sectoral ETFs have a lesser weighting (the planets) and the more niche ETFs are your smallest holdings (the moon).

Once your skills and knowledge improves, you may want to consider using options so that you can hedge against potential downside risks, generate income through covered calls and speculate on price movements. I explain this strategy in greater depth in the next chapter.

## 5-POINT ACTION PLAN

1. Take the time to understand the concepts behind ETFs and their benefits. Learn about the different types of ETFs, their underlying assets and their investment strategies.
2. Carefully consider your investment objectives and risk tolerance. Decide whether you want to focus on long-term growth, income generation, or specific market sectors.
3. Select a reputable ETF provider by evaluating their offerings, fees, liquidity and track records.
4. Build a diversified portfolio by implementing the 'solar system' investment model, where your largest holding represents broad market indices, your mid-sized holdings are smaller sectoral ETFs, and your smallest holdings are niche ETFs.
5. As you gain experience and knowledge, consider incorporating options trading to enhance your ETF strategies. Learn about using options to hedge against potential downside risks, generate additional income through covered calls, and capitalise on price movements.

## ONLINE RESOURCES

Learning how to create and manage a portfolio of Exchange Traded Funds could well be the backbone of your investment plan. Make sure you check out the free workshop at wealthplaybook.com.au before kicking off your ETF portfolio.

# Chapter 16

# EXOTICS

Speculation without knowledge is mere gambling.

Jesse Livermore

In the hustle and bustle of daily life, you might drive a sturdy Toyota Camry – a champion of practicality and economic sensibility. It gets you where you need to go efficiently and reliably.

In your garage, however, imagine that you have a beautiful, yet temperamental vintage Porsche. It guzzles huge amounts of fuel and isn't necessarily the safest or most reliable set of wheels, but it's flashy, fun and guarantees a thrilling weekend drive.

As you begin your investment journey, think of the Camry as your 'safe haven' investments – your exchange-traded funds, shares and real estate. Combined, they should be your primary vehicle for navigating the long and steady trip from where you are now to where you want to be.

The Porsche, on the other hand, symbolises 'exotic' financial products such as cryptocurrencies, exchange-traded options and forex trading platforms. They can give you an adrenaline rush and get you places quickly, but are fraught with unpredictability and risk. If you choose only the exotic vehicles, you're likely to face more breakdowns, detours and crashes.

Your investment portfolio definitely has room for both metaphorical cars. However, just like I would caution against purchasing a sports car before owning an everyday sedan, I recommend only exploring volatile exotic investment opportunities once you have your more basic investment structures in place. This idea is captured in the following figure.

### Understanding The Risk Pyramid

**High-risk investment:**
foreign exchange trading, CFDs, cryptocurrencies, exchange-trading options

Speculation

**Moderate risk investment:**
blue chip stocks, growth stocks, real estate, mutual funds, royalty trusts.

Growth

**Low-risk investment:**
corporate bonds, government bonds, treasury securities

Safety and income

*Increasing potential for high returns*
*Increasing risk*

**Cash and cash equivalents:**
savings accounts, certificates of deposit, treasury bills, insurance

Financial security

Once you're at this point and ready to commit a small percentage of your portfolio to the exotics, it's important to know how they work – and that's what I explain in this chapter. Hopefully by the end, you'll know the basics of how to safely drive that Porsche!

## FOREIGN EXCHANGE (FOREX) TRADING

Foreign exchange trading, also known as 'forex' or 'FX trading', is one of the most speculative and volatile forms of investing. It involves buying and selling different currencies in the global market, with the aim of profiting from changes in exchange rates.

Currencies are always traded in pairs – for example, the Euro and the US dollar (represented as EUR/USD), or the British pound and the Japanese yen (GBP/JPY). The first currency in the pair is the 'base' currency, and the second is the 'quote' currency.

If you believe that the base currency will rise against the quote currency, you would 'buy' the pair. If you believe it will fall, you would 'sell'.

The forex market is the largest and most liquid financial market in the world, with a daily trading volume in the trillions of dollars. It operates 24 hours a day, five days a week, which means you can react to global economic events as they happen.

## LESSON BLOCK: FOREX FUNDAMENTALS

If you're planning to delve into the high-stakes world of forex trading, it's important to understand the many factors that can influence a currency's value at any given time. These include:

- *Economic indicators:* These include data points such as employment figures, GDP growth, inflation rates, retail sales and manufacturing output.
- *Monetary policy decisions:* Central banks play a key role in currency value through the setting of interest rates. When a central bank raises interest rates, its currency often strengthens due to the potential for higher returns. Conversely, when a central bank lowers interest rates, its currency can weaken.
- *Geopolitical events:* Political stability is key to a strong currency. Events such as elections, political transitions, wars or conflicts can lead to uncertainty and volatility in the currency markets.
- *Market sentiment:* The overall mood of investors can drive the value of currencies. If investors feel optimistic about a particular currency, they will buy it and its value will increase. If they feel pessimistic, they will sell, and its value will decrease.

Forex trading involves dealing with extremely small currency movements, known as pips (a thousandth of a percent). This means that traders usually need to use leverage to capitalise on the minute fluctuations.

Leverage in forex trading is essentially a loan provided by the broker that allows traders to control large positions with a relatively small amount of capital. This amplifies the potential for profit, because even small shifts in exchange rates can translate to significant returns.

However, it's important to remember that while leverage can magnify profits, it can also exacerbate losses. If the market moves against a leveraged position, the potential loss could exceed the initial investment. Therefore, risk management strategies, including the use of stop-loss orders and carefully monitoring market trends, are crucial.

As always, it's important to educate yourself about the risks and only trade with funds that you can afford to lose. These days the internet is littered with forex brokers promising a quick path to financial freedom – but such claims are often misleading.

The forex market is a professional playground dominated by high-frequency traders and algorithmic trading systems. Attempting to compete with such giants can result in being outmanoeuvred (for example, where trading skips past your stop-loss before it can be filled) and sustaining heavy losses.

Many people are also unaware that forex trading has its own industry peculiarities, such as the 'B-Book' method, which sees your broker take the opposite position to your trade. The logic behind this practice is tied to the statistical reality that a significant majority of retail forex traders tend to lose money. By employing the B-Book method, brokers potentially stand to profit from those client losses.

Although this is not illegal and is often disclosed in the small print of agreements, it raises ethical questions and underscores the importance of conducting thorough research and choosing a reliable and regulated broker.

Overall, it's important to remember that while forex trading can play a part in a diversified trading strategy, it is a highly speculative tool and comes with many challenges and risks. Tread carefully!

## CFDS (CONTRACTS FOR DIFFERENCE)

A contract for difference (CFD) is a type of derivative that allows you to speculate on the price movements in share prices, stock market indexes, foreign exchange rates, and many other assets.

What makes the process different from simply buying the asset, however, is that you don't need to stump up the full price upfront. Instead, you enter into a contract with a CFD provider to exchange the difference in the price of the underlying asset from the contract's opening to its closure.

Often, you will only need to pay a small amount of the asset's actual price (known as 'initial margin') to enter the trade. For example, say you are purchasing 100 shares in a company with a share price of $25.26. If buying the shares outright, this would cost you $2526 (plus brokerage fees). If you purchase via a CFD, however, you may only need to pay the provider 5 per cent of that amount up-front, which equates to $126.30. If the share price increases by 50c per share and you exit the trade at that point, you will have made $50 profit on your $126.30 initial investment, or a 39.5 per cent profit.

The table on the following page shows you the difference between this method and buying the stock outright from a traditional broker in more detail.

It's important to note the table doesn't factor in brokerage fees or the cost of the spreads and fees applied by the CFD broker; however, you can see the return on investment in percentage terms is significantly higher via CFDs than if you'd bought the stock at full price from a traditional broker.

The risk, however, is that the stock price will drop below the initial ask price. The next table shows that if the share price fell to $24.62, you would suddenly be facing a loss of more than 50 per cent on your initial investment.

Keep in mind the preceding table shows losses for a drop in the share price of just 64 cents. The trade can become even scarier when the value of the shares fall by an amount greater than the initial

## CFDs: The Impact of Leverage

| Transaction | Traditional stock broker | CFD broker |
|---|---|---|
| Ask price of the stock | $25.26 | $25.26 |
| Number of shares bought | 100 | 100 |
| Total transaction cost | $2526 | $2526 |
| Required upfront capital | $2526 (100% of transaction cost) | $126.30 (5% margin) |
| Selling price and profit | $2576 ($50 profit) | $2576 ($50 profit) |
| Return on investment | $50 ÷ $2526 = 1.98% | $50 ÷ $126.30 = 39.5% |

| Transaction | Traditional stock broker | CFD broker |
|---|---|---|
| Ask price of the stock | $25.26 | $25.26 |
| Number of shares bought | 100 | 100 |
| Total transaction cost | $2526 | $2526 |
| Required upfront capital | $2526 (100% of transaction cost) | $126.30 (5% margin) |
| Selling price and loss | $2462 ($64 loss) | $2462 ($64 loss) |
| Return on investment | $64 ÷ $2526 = –2.53% | $64 ÷ $126.30 = –50.67% |

margin you'd provided to the broker. In such a scenario, you may face a situation known as a 'margin call', where the broker requires you to deposit additional funds (known as 'variation margin') to cover the losses. If you don't provide these extra funds, you risk having your positions forcibly closed. The following table shows that a 16 per cent fall in a share price in the same example trade would equate to a 321 per cent loss on your initial investment!

| Transaction | Traditional stock broker | CFD broker |
|---|---|---|
| Ask price of the stock | $25.26 | $25.26 |
| Number of shares bought | 100 | 100 |
| Total transaction cost | $2526 | $2526 |
| Required upfront capital | $2526 (100% of transaction cost) | $126.30 (5% margin) |
| Selling price and loss | $2120 ($406 loss) | $2120 ($406 loss) |
| Return on investment | $406 ÷ $2526 = −16.07% | $406 ÷ $126.30 = −321.47% |

This example isn't aimed at scaring you away from CFDs. They can be an effective financial instrument, and many traders find them particularly useful when looking to take short positions on particular assets – in other words, looking to profit from a falling share price.

However, it is important to highlight how risky CFDs can be and why they should only be traded by those with sufficient experience and knowledge.

## CRYPTOCURRENCIES

It would be remiss of me to write a chapter about exotic investments without mentioning the most speculative of them all!

Cryptocurrencies and online payment systems, such as Bitcoin and Ethereum, have gained significant attention in recent years for their potential for explosive gains and losses. Their decentralised nature, technological complexities and the influence of market sentiment make them an intriguing investment option.

The advent of Bitcoin in 2009 definitely caused a seismic shift around the world. Millions of people who'd previously found investing boring and cumbersome were suddenly attracted to this new, fast and exciting way to trade. As a result, many of those people have since also taken the time to learn about more traditional markets – and that's a good thing.

However, I have to say I am not a huge fan of cryptocurrencies for two main reasons. Firstly, the entire industry around the creation and trading of the new 'digital money' lacks regulation and oversight. This exposes investors to fraud, scams and market manipulation.

We have seen investors lose billions of dollars through events such as the Mt. Gox exchange hack in 2014, where approximately 850,000 bitcoins were stolen, and the Bitconnect scheme, which promised high returns through a lending and trading platform but was exposed as a Ponzi scheme in 2018.

More recently, in 2022, the Bahamas-based cryptocurrency exchange FTX went bankrupt, leaving more than a million customers out of pocket. It justified the view of many from within the traditional investing world who refer to the crypto space as the 'wild west'.

My second primary concern about cryptocurrencies is that many claims touted by their proponents simply aren't true. They will tell you, for example, that bitcoin is a safe place to turn in times of turbulence in other markets. So far, we have seen the opposite. Instead, crypto has shown significant correlation to the Dow Jones index and has not proven itself as a reliable inflation hedge.

Another claim they make is that cryptocurrencies act as a store of wealth. Over certain timeframes, that has been somewhat true for bitcoin, but other cryptocurrencies have been unreliable to say the very least. Terra Luna and Solana are examples of the so-called coins that dropped billions of dollars in market cap in a flash.

Some examples exist of cryptocurrencies being usable for transactions, but their adoption for payments has been slow. So far, the main reason people have bought them is to strike it rich. Some have succeeded, some have failed. Fortunes have been made and fortunes have been lost.

One potential game changer in this space could be a gold-backed cryptocurrency, combining a speculative tool with a tangible store of wealth. Such an innovation could turn things around for the crypto market, and people smarter than me are working on this at the time of writing.

For now, however, cryptocurrencies represent the apex of speculation, and are akin to going to the races and giving your money to a bookie.

## EXCHANGE-TRADED OPTIONS

I'm going to finish the chapter with one of my favourite investment tools.

Exchange-traded options, also referred to as ETOs, are financial derivatives that provide investors with the right, but not the obligation, to buy or sell a particular asset at a predetermined price, known as the 'strike price', before or on a specific date.

As the name suggests, these options are traded on exchanges. They're popular for their flexibility and potential for high returns, but they also carry significant risks.

There are two types of options: call options and put options. The characteristics of the two types are defined in the following table.

## Call and Put Options

| Option type | Right granted | Investor's expectation |
|---|---|---|
| Call option | The right to buy an asset at a specific price within a certain period | The investor expects the price of the underlying asset to increase |
| Put option | The right to sell an asset at a specific price within a certain period | The investor expects the price of the underlying asset to decrease |

When you buy an option, whether it's a call or a put, you pay what is known as a 'premium'. The premium is the price of the option itself, and is determined by several factors, including the price of the underlying asset, the strike price of the option, the time until the option expires, and the volatility of the underlying asset. These may be new terms for you to understand and training is essential before investing in options.

The premium is paid upfront when you buy the option and represents your maximum potential loss. The premium is multiplied by the number of shares the option contract represents. In most markets, including the United States, one option contract typically represents 100 shares of the underlying asset. So if an option has a premium of $1, buying one contract would cost you $100 ($1 × 100 shares).

As mentioned, the option gives buyers the *right* to buy or sell by a certain date – but not the *obligation*. If the underlying share price doesn't move in the direction the options buyer thought it would, they can simply let the contract expire without doing anything. This means the upfront premium is the maximum amount the option buyer can lose. However, the potential profit for an option buyer can be quite substantial if the price of the underlying asset does move in the direction they anticipated.

## LESSON BLOCK: OPTIONS EXAMPLE

To illustrate how options work, let's imagine Netflix is currently trading at $500 per share and you believe that the price will rise in the next three months. You decide to buy a call option with a strike price of $520 that expires in three months. The premium for this option is $10 per share.

Since one options contract typically represents 100 shares, the total cost of buying this call option would be $1000 (100 shares × $10 per share premium).

Here are two possible outcomes:

- *Netflix shares rise above $520 (the strike price):* Let's say Netflix shares rise to $550. Your call option allows you to buy shares for $520, which means you're making a profit of $30 per share ($550 market price – $520 strike price). However, you paid a $10 premium per share, so your net profit per share is $20 ($30 profit – $10 premium). Therefore, your total profit for the contract would be $2000 ($20 profit per share × 100 shares).

- *Netflix shares stay at or below $520:* If the Netflix share price doesn't rise above the strike price of $520 by the expiration date, the option becomes worthless. You don't exercise the option because you can buy the shares cheaper on the open market. In this case, you lose the entire premium paid, which is $1000.

Your maximum loss is always just the cost of the premium but your potential profit is theoretically unlimited.

Keep in mind that actual trading can be more complex. Prices can change rapidly, and you also need to consider trading fees. This example also assumes you exercise the option and immediately sell the shares, which may not always be the case.

I've dedicated the past three decades of my career to derivatives, with a special fondness for options. They not only can be used for speculation, but also are a powerful risk management tool because they allow investors to hedge their positions, limiting potential losses on other investments.

For example, an investor who owns a stock and fears its price might fall can buy a put option, effectively 'insuring' their shares. If the stock price then falls, the put option increases in value, offsetting the loss from the stock. This is an extremely powerful benefit to using options, in that it provides peace of mind – a mile away from the risk that most uneducated people associate with options trading.

Similarly, you can generate income by using a 'covered calls' strategy, which allows you to profit from stocks you already own. By selling a covered call, you offer someone the right to buy your stock at a certain price, known as the strike price, within a specific time frame.

You receive a premium immediately for selling this option. If the stock's price stays below the strike price by the expiration date, the option won't be exercised, and you get to keep both your stock and the premium. (Almost like having your cake and eating it too.) However, if the stock's price rises above the strike price, you may have to sell your stock but you still keep the premium.

This system of selling a covered call on stock you own is the basis of my Cashflow on Demand strategy, which I mention throughout this book. The strategy can be a consistent way to generate income, especially in a flat or slightly rising market. The only downside is it limits the potential upside if the price of your stock rises significantly (and you need to sell it). Again, this is a more advanced strategy that you should only undertake once you fully understand it, and the risks involved.

So, for the reasons outlined in this section, I am a big advocate of exchange traded options, but you do need to learn how to use them properly. Investing in your education is paramount to unlocking the potential that options can provide in your investment journey.

## DRIVE SAFELY

Now that you have the keys to the Porsche, it doesn't necessarily mean you should hit the highway. Exotics do have their place in investment portfolios, but I can't stress enough how important it is to be careful. Remember, the journey of wealth creation is a long-term endeavour that requires patience and persistence.

### 5-POINT ACTION PLAN

1. Prioritise education and research to understand the nuances and risks associated with exotic investments. Explore reputable sources, attend seminars or webinars, and read books or articles written by experts in the field.
2. Ensure you have built a well-diversified portfolio of safer investments such as exchange-traded funds, shares and real estate before dabbling in exotic investments.
3. Approach cryptocurrencies with caution and conduct thorough research on their underlying technology and potential use cases before investing. Be aware of the risk and only invest what you can afford to lose.
4. If interested in options trading, dedicate time to understanding the mechanics and strategies involved. Learn about call and put options, premiums, strike prices and expiration dates. Australian Investment Education offers training and guidance to help you build confidence in using this investment tool effectively.
5. Strive for a well-rounded investment portfolio that combines the stability of traditional investments with the potential growth offered by exotic options.

## ONLINE RESOURCES

Exotics can deliver a great value add to investment portfolios. Our free training on their role at wealthplaybook.com.au will help you incorporate them into your plan in a lower risk, value add way.

# Chapter 17

# BONDS

Bonds should come with a warning label.

Warren Buffett

If you've turned to this chapter hoping to read about Daniel Craig, Sean Connery and Roger Moore, or even the iconic Australian underwear brand, I have bad news. Bonds in the finance world are nowhere near as fun and glamorous. However, when traded correctly, they can make you solid returns.

The easiest way to understand bonds is to think of them like an IOU. Just as you'd lend a friend $5 to buy a coffee, you can lend much larger sums of money to corporations or governments. In return, they provide you with a bond certificate, which represents their promise to repay the principal amount at the bond's maturity, which could be in 12 months or even 50 years.

In addition to the repayment of the principal, bonds also pay periodic interest, known as 'coupon payments', to bondholders. This interest rate is determined at the time of issuance and remains fixed throughout the bond's life. By holding bonds until maturity, investors can earn a predictable income stream alongside the return of their initial investment.

In most cases, the risk to the investor is low, and the interest rates can be enticing. However, Warren Buffett once said bonds should 'come with a warning label' for a reason – and I generally don't hold them in my portfolio.

Like all investment products, they are the right fit for some, but not for others. In this chapter, I give you all the information you need to decide whether bonds belong in your portfolio.

## HOW BONDS WORK

To illustrate how bonds make you returns, let's use the example of a toll roads company seeking funding to construct a new highway. In order to raise the necessary funds, the company offers bonds to investors.

John, a conservative investor with spare cash to deploy, takes the opportunity to buy a 10-year, $10,000 bond with annual interest of 5 per cent. On each year for those 10 years, John will receive $500 in passive income, totalling $5000. At the conclusion of the term, he will also be given back his initial $10,000 investment. He now has a total of $15,000.

In this instance, John has taken on minimal risk because the toll company has a proven track record and has government backing to help improve the road network. However, not all bonds are created equal.

## BOND RISKS

You probably have friends you would lend money to and others that you wouldn't – and bond investing can be much the same!

There is a chance that the corporation or government you lend the money to will never give it back. If the issuer defaults or becomes insolvent, you could be out of pocket the entire amount you invested. This is more likely to happen if you lend the money to an early-stage company than, say, the United States Government, which can just print more money to pay its debts.

It's also important to be aware that if you decide to sell your bond before it reaches maturity, its price may be higher or lower than your initial investment. The reason for this is that bond prices are influenced by various factors, and I cover these in the following sections.

### Interest rates

When market interest rates decrease, bonds with higher fixed returns become more attractive to investors. This increased demand causes the price of these bonds to rise, because investors are willing to pay more for the higher yield.

Conversely, when market interest rates increase, bonds with lower fixed returns become less attractive, resulting in decreased demand and lower bond prices.

This is captured in the following figure.

**The Impact of Interest Rates on Bonds**

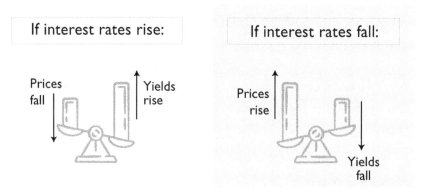

To illustrate in more detail how this works, the table on the following page shows an expected change in value for the toll road company's $10,000 bond used in the earlier example.

### Inflation

Inflation directly impacts bond prices through its effect on the purchasing power of what you're earning on your investment. For example, if you invest $100 in a bond today and receive $100 back

**Bond prices and Interest Rates**

| Market interest rate | Bond coupon | Bond attractiveness | Bond price |
|---|---|---|---|
| 3% | 5% | More attractive | $12,000 |
| 4% | 5% | More attractive | $11,000 |
| 5% | 5% | Neutral | $10,000 |
| 6% | 5% | Less attractive | $9,000 |
| 7% | 5% | Less attractive | $8,000 |

in five years, the purchasing power of that $100 may have diminished significantly, perhaps to the equivalent of only $60 to $70 in today's money.

When inflation is high, your fixed interest payments also become less valuable. So if you're receiving 5 per cent interest, but inflation is 6 per cent, you're actually getting a negative real return of 1 per cent. This makes bonds less attractive during times of inflation and, as such, when inflation rises, bond prices generally fall.

## Credit ratings

Another factor that will significantly impact a bond's price is its perceived credit risk. Unlike with stocks, organisations such as Standard & Poor's (S&P) rate the quality of bonds by assigning a credit rating to a borrower, so you know how likely it is that you'll get your expected payments.

In general, the higher the credit rating, the more likely an issuer will make its interest payments and repay the principal on a bond. This means that if the issuer's credit rating falls, its bond price will also fall, and vice versa. It's also important to note that lower risk usually means lower returns and, therefore, the better the borrower's credit rating, the lower the fixed interest rate of the bond.

If you're going to go down the path of buying bonds, it is very important to assess credit ratings, but also look out for any conflicts of interest. For example, during the global financial crisis, it was revealed that bond issuers pay rating agencies to evaluate their credit profiles, which led to concerns their assessments were biased.

## LESSON BLOCK: TYPES OF BONDS

The following table outlines the different types of bonds and their risk levels.

| Type of bond | Issuer | Description | Risk level |
|---|---|---|---|
| Government bonds | National governments | • Low-risk investments backed by the government<br>• Lower yields due to lower risk<br>• Includes Treasury Bonds (T-Bonds), Treasury Notes (T-Notes), and Treasury Bills (T-Bills), with varying maturities from less than a year to 30 years | Low |
| Municipal bonds | State, provincial or local governments | • Bonds financing public projects such as infrastructure, schools or hospitals<br>• May offer tax advantages<br>• Includes General Obligation Bonds (GO Bonds) backed by the full faith and credit of the issuing municipality, and Revenue Bonds tied to specific projects or revenue sources | Low to moderate |

| Type of bond | Issuer | Description | Risk level |
|---|---|---|---|
| Corporate bonds | Corporations | • Bonds issued by corporations to raise capital for business operations or expansions<br>• Higher yields than government or municipal bonds<br>• Includes Investment-Grade Corporate Bonds issued by corporations with strong credit ratings and High-Yield Corporate Bonds (Junk Bonds) issued by corporations with lower credit ratings | Moderate to high |
| Secured bonds | Various issuers | • Bonds backed by specific assets, such as mortgages or other collateral<br>• Provides added security to investors in case of issuer default<br>• Includes Mortgage-Backed Securities (MBS) with interest and principal payments derived from mortgage payments made by borrowers, and Asset-Backed Securities (ABS) backed by non-mortgage assets such as auto loans or credit card receivables | Moderate |
| Zero-coupon bonds | Various issuers | • Bonds issued at a discount to their face value and redeemed at full face value upon maturity<br>• Do not pay periodic interest<br>• The difference between the purchase price and the face value represents the bond's return | Varies |

## TRADING BONDS

As mentioned, you can buy and sell bonds after their initial issuance in the primary market. Various channels allow the trading process, such as over-the-counter (OTC) markets, electronic trading platforms, or bond brokers and dealers. However, the OTC market is the most common venue, because many bonds are not listed on formal exchanges.

As with all investments, it's important to assess the liquidity of the market you're trading in. Some bonds, such as those issued by the US Treasury, are highly liquid because of their large market size and strong demand from investors.

Other bonds, such as corporate or municipal bonds, may be less liquid, making it more challenging to find a buyer or seller at your desired price. Lower liquidity can result in a wider gap between the bid–ask spreads, which is the difference between the highest price a buyer is willing to pay (bid) and the lowest price a seller is willing to accept (ask).

## INVESTING THROUGH BOND FUNDS

My preferred method of trading the bond market is through exchange-traded funds (ETFs – refer to chapter 15). These funds pool contributions from investors and use this pool to purchase a diversified portfolio of bonds. This diversification helps mitigate the risks associated with individual bonds, such as credit risk and issuer-specific events.

Another advantage of trading bonds through ETFs is the ease of access and liquidity. Bond ETFs are listed on stock exchanges and can be bought and sold throughout the trading day, just like stocks.

This trading flexibility allows investors to react more quickly to market movements, and the generally higher liquidity of ETFs compared to individual bonds can lead to tighter bid–ask spreads and lower transaction costs.

Bond ETFs can also offer a more transparent pricing mechanism compared to individual bonds. The ETF's market price reflects the value of its underlying bond portfolio, which is typically updated throughout the trading day. In contrast, when trading individual bonds, the OTC market can make it more challenging to determine the fair market value, because price information may be less readily available.

However, it is important to note that investing in bond ETFs also has its drawbacks. For instance, fees are associated with ETFs, such as management fees and trading commissions, which investors need to consider.

Additionally, bond ETFs may not always perfectly replicate the performance of their underlying bond portfolios due to tracking errors or other factors. Nonetheless, for many investors, the benefits of trading bonds through ETFs, such as diversification, ease of access and transparency, can outweigh the potential drawbacks.

## ARE BONDS RIGHT FOR YOU?

So why did Warren Buffett describe bonds as 'the most dangerous of assets'? Because, he argued, they offer low returns compared to equities and 'destroy the purchasing power' of investors. I have also avoided bonds throughout my investing journey because I prefer to seek higher gains from the stock market by using my skills and experience in trading.

However, for more passive investors, bonds can be an excellent source of regular cash flow. My father, for example, enjoys the relative safety and consistency of bonds. As a widower who travels frequently, he enjoys the predictability of his monthly income, which helps him budget effectively.

Whether or not bonds are right for you will depend on your risk profile, age, skill-set and personal circumstances. If you prefer a lower risk investment, protection against market volatility or a stable income stream in retirement, then bonds could be a great option. But if you are younger and wanting to achieve financial freedom as quickly as possible, you could be better served elsewhere.

## 5-POINT ACTION PLAN

1. Determine if bonds are the right fit for your investment strategy. Consider factors such as your age, risk tolerance and financial objectives.
2. Familiarise yourself with different types of bonds and evaluate their respective risk levels and potential returns. Check the credit ratings assigned by rating agencies to gauge the credit-worthiness of bond issuers.
3. Decide whether you want to invest in individual bonds directly via the issuer, or through investing in bond exchange-traded funds (ETFs). Consider factors such as diversification, liquidity and transaction costs associated with each method.
4. Keep an eye on interest rates and inflation because these factors can impact bond prices and should help inform your trading decisions.
5. Keep yourself updated on the latest developments in the bond market and the broader economic landscape. Read financial news, follow market trends and better educate yourself where necessary.

## ONLINE RESOURCES

Check out the online Success Portal at wealthplaybook.com.au for more on bonds.

# Chapter 18

# YOUR HOME

A man's home is his castle.

Darryl Kerrigan (Michael Caton)

Few financial decisions carry as much weight as purchasing a place to call home. For the majority of people, it will be the most important investment they ever make. And for that reason, it can also be the biggest source of stress!

Unlike the transactional nature of buying shares or other investment products, the process of securing a home can carry deep emotional significance. It's not just about crunching numbers and assessing market trends; it's also about finding a place that reflects our identity, meets our needs and fulfils our aspirations. We seek a place where we can build a life, create memories and find solace at the end of each day.

Many Australians, particularly of my generation, will be familiar with the quote under the heading of this chapter, which comes from the iconic 1997 movie *The Castle*. Darryl Kerrigan, played by actor Michael Caton, proclaimed 'a man's home is his castle' as he fought to save his modest weatherboard from the threat of being lost to a nearby airport expansion.

While the movie is somewhat satirical, the quote, which actually derives from similar words said by English judge Sir Edward Coke in 1644, emphasises the idea that our homes are more than just financial assets or physical structures – they are our personal fortresses, our safe havens where we can truly be ourselves.

Kerrigan also refers to the home as being his family's 'patch of paradise' and says that 'no amount of money' can replace the memories they've made in the place. It's a reminder that the true worth of a home often goes beyond its monetary value and highlights why when buying or selling real estate, emotion can very easily take over rationality.

In this chapter, I outline the factors you should consider – and those you should ignore – when it comes to buying your principal place of residence (PPR).

If you get it right, you can not only have the pleasure of living in a beautiful home in a great location, but also land yourself an incredible financial investment. History has shown house prices typically appreciate over time, and in some cases the capital gains can be life-changing.

## CHOOSING YOUR HOME

Selecting your first home, or deciding on your next one, can be a daunting process. Your friends, family and work colleagues will undoubtedly be keen to share their wisdom on what you should buy, where you should buy and how much you should spend.

Be aware that their advice, while well meaning, can sometimes add to the noise and confusion. It's usually best to sideline this external chatter and instead concentrate your mental and emotional energy on the three key buying criteria covered in the following sections.

## Affordability

The allure of acquiring your dream home can often entice you to push your financial boundaries to their limit. However, it's essential to prioritise affordability as a key factor in your decision-making process.

For most home buyers, taking out a mortgage will be a necessary evil, but you can control how much debt you take on by being sensible about your choice of property. The following table shows how scary your repayments can become if you end up with a large mortgage and a high interest rate. (The table shows principle and interest repayments on a 30-year loan.)

**The impact of interest rates on affordability**

| Loan amount | Monthly repayment at 2% annual interest | Monthly repayment at 4% annual interest | Monthly repayment at 6% annual interest | Monthly repayment at 8% annual interest | Monthly repayment at 10% annual interest |
|---|---|---|---|---|---|
| $200,000 | $739 | $955 | $1199 | $1468 | $1755 |
| $400,000 | $1478 | $1910 | $2398 | $2935 | $3510 |
| $600,000 | $2218 | $2864 | $3597 | $4403 | $5265 |
| $800,000 | $2957 | $3819 | $4796 | $5870 | $7021 |
| $1,000,000 | $3696 | $4774 | $5996 | $7338 | $8776 |

Before choosing a home, carefully evaluate your ability to service your mortgage should interest rates increase significantly. To give yourself an extra level of comfort when borrowing, the following formula may assist you.

If interest rates are above their eight-year average at the time of taking out the loan, factor in being able to make repayments with interest rates being 2 per cent more than what you are being offered. Alternatively, if interest rates are below their eight-year average, factor in being able to make repayments with interest rates being

4 per cent more than what you are being offered, to ensure you have a sufficient buffer.

So, while you may feel comfortable with the $2854 monthly payment that comes with borrowing $600,000 at 4 per cent, if interest rates are below their eight-year average, you also need to consider whether you could continue to meet payments of $4403 at 8 per cent.

Factoring in as much as a 4 per cent increase may sound extreme, but economic conditions can change rapidly and should you suddenly find yourself failing to meet your obligations, your property could be repossessed. Even coming close to that situation would cause significant distress and many sleepless nights.

Opting for a more modestly priced home will also provide you with the financial flexibility needed to adapt to life events, such as the arrival of children, and enable you to pay your mortgage off quicker so you can turn your attention to other investments. As my father always wisely advised, 'If you owe people money, you never own your life.' It's an old-school view, but it has served me well.

It's also important to remember that, unlike with investment properties, you're not able to claim mortgage interest as a tax deduction when dealing with a primary residence. This means that the financial burden of the loan falls entirely on you.

## Functionality

In the miserable depths of the COVID-19 pandemic, most of us became acutely aware of the drawbacks of living in a home where the occupants' needs have changed beyond what the property can offer. Many who were previously content living in small city apartments suddenly found themselves needing more space for remote work. As a result, larger houses became increasingly attractive.

While it's obviously hard to foresee events like a pandemic, it does pay to think about how your housing needs might change as time goes on. This foresight can help you avoid needing to purchase another home in the near or mid-term future.

Couples preparing to have children might look for houses with a safe outdoor play area and bedrooms that are close together, while buyers approaching retirement might prioritise low-maintenance, single-story homes with mobility-friendly features.

Certainly, you can always upgrade your home as your lifestyle changes, but such a choice comes with substantial financial implications. Between agents' fees and stamp duty, you could end up shelling out tens of thousands of dollars. For this reason, it's wise to approach real estate investments with a long lens.

---

### LESSON BLOCK: FUNCTIONALITY CHECKLIST

Before purchasing a new home, take some time to consider how the following factors may impact its functionality now and into the future:

- *Space requirement:* Consider the number of bedrooms, bathrooms and other living spaces you currently need and may require in the future.
- *Home office:* If you work from home or anticipate doing so, you might need a dedicated and quiet workspace.
- *Internet connectivity:* Ensure the area has reliable high-speed internet, especially if you depend on it for work or entertainment.
- *Kitchen layout and appliances:* Depending on your cooking habits, you might want a modern, spacious kitchen with quality appliances.
- *Outdoor space:* If you enjoy gardening, entertaining or simply being outdoors, a yard, balcony or patio might be essential.
- *Parking:* Confirm the property comes with adequate parking for your family's vehicles.
- *Storage space:* Storage spaces such as closets, attics, basements or garages can help keep your home uncluttered.

- *Natural light:* A well-lit home can make spaces appear larger and more inviting.
- *Energy efficiency:* Energy-efficient homes can save you money on utility bills and help the environment.
- *Heating and cooling systems:* Depending on the climate, a good air conditioning system can significantly increase comfort.
- *Potential for expansion:* If you might need more space in the future, check whether the property allows for additions or renovations.
- *Maintenance and repair costs:* Older homes might have more character but could also require more maintenance and repairs.

## Location

The old adage 'location, location, location' is popular in real estate for a reason. A great location can improve your quality of life and ensure the value of your home increases over time. This is why you may have been given advice to buy the 'worst house on the best street'. The logic being that you can always renovate a home, but you can't pick it up and move it to another suburb!

When it comes to choosing your location, here are the factors you should consider:

- *Commute and accessibility:* Proximity to public transport is a factor that many buyers overlook, but can have an enormous impact on a property's value. A 2016 research study found that Sydney homes located within 400 metres of a train station enjoy an average 4.5 per cent premium in land value. The importance of easy transport access tends to shift through various stages of life. During our younger years, trains, buses and trams can be crucial for our daily commute. However, as we age, the focus can shift towards being close to well-maintained roads and airports.

- *Amenities:* The proximity to essential services and recreational facilities can make life easier and more enjoyable. Houses that are close to supermarkets, schools, hospitals, restaurants and sporting stadiums will enhance your lifestyle and generally increase in value.

- *Community and neighbourhood:* A friendly and vibrant neighbourhood can boost your mental and emotional wellbeing. A great location often means a great community, which can be especially important for families with children.

- *Future development:* It also pays to investigate which locations might be slated for future development or improvement. New hospitals, schools, roads and public transport networks can significantly increase your property's value over time.

- *Safety:* Crime rates also come into play when evaluating a location's suitability. Living in an inner-city area with a rough reputation may be acceptable for some, especially when affordability is a significant factor. However, if you're starting a young family or looking to retire, a safe neighbourhood will be high on your list of priorities.

- *Personal taste:* It's important to remember that what constitutes a 'great location' can be subjective and depends largely on individual needs and preferences. Some people may prioritise living close to the city centre, while others may prefer the quiet of the suburbs. Similarly, one person might prefer an area with a bustling nightlife, while another might want proximity to parks and outdoor spaces.

Ultimately, the right location will align with your personal lifestyle and financial goals. As mentioned earlier, if you are looking for an affordable home it's likely you will need to make compromises.

## GET STARTED!

The sooner you can acquire a home that you can call your own, whether through mortgage payments or outright ownership, the better. It becomes a valuable asset that then supports your other wealth creation endeavours.

The earlier you throw down an anchor into the property market, the longer your investments have to grow and accumulate wealth. While renting may offer certain benefits, ultimately it means paying for something you don't own.

It's important to let go of the belief that you can't afford to buy and instead focus on what you can afford. While you may not be able to purchase your dream property in the most desirable area right away, over time, you will move closer to your dream destination. Also consider what improvements you can make to the property once purchased. These could range from working on the landscaping to planning some renovations, and could be completed over the short or longer term. These changes can not only make the property more liveable for you, but also increase its capital growth potential.

Remember, if you never start, you'll never get there.

# 5-POINT ACTION PLAN

1. Evaluate your financial capabilities, understand the implications of borrowing money and calculate how much you could afford for mortgage payments each month. Consider potential interest rate fluctuations in your calculations to ensure you can handle future increases.

2. Reflect on your current lifestyle and envision how it might change in the future. This should inform the kind of house you need, factoring in aspects such as the number of rooms, the size of any outdoor space and provision for a home office.

3. Research potential locations based on their proximity to essential amenities, crime rates and public transportation options. Assess these factors from both a present and future perspective, considering how your needs may evolve over time.

4. As soon as you're financially ready, start the process of acquiring your own home. This investment can grow over time and contribute to your wealth creation journey. Consider making compromises on less crucial factors to expedite this step if necessary.

5. Once you secure a property, consider value-adding improvements such as renovations or landscaping that can increase your home's value and appeal. Strategically investing in these improvements could significantly enhance your property's future sale prospects.

## ONLINE RESOURCES

Check out the online Success Portal at wealthplaybook.com.au for more on your home.

# Chapter 19

# INVESTMENT PROPERTIES

Don't wait to buy real estate. Buy real estate and wait.
Will Rogers

The previous chapter explained why a place to call home is usually a sound, long-term investment. However, building serious wealth through real estate typically requires going beyond that first purchase and acquiring properties that you rent out to others – a strategy that's proven lucrative for millions of investors around the world.

People are attracted to the idea of owning investment properties because they're tangible assets that you can see, touch and have direct control over. They provide a sense of security and stability that often doesn't come with shares and most other investment products.

What's more, property provides opportunities for significant financial gains in the form of regular rental income and property value growth. These earnings can come without the need for huge amounts of upfront cash because lenders typically offer favourable financing options for real estate. Better still, the interest payments on your loan can be used as a tax deduction.

It all sounds quite compelling, but being a landlord does come with a unique set of risks and challenges. You need to find and vet tenants, deal with repairs and disputes, and ensure compliance with local regulations. While these tasks can be outsourced to a property management company, doing so will incur additional costs that must be factored into your planning.

The following figure highlights some of the factors to consider when investing in real estate.

**Decision Markers for Investment Property**

In this chapter, I guide you through some of these complexities and provide you with the tools and insights needed to become a successful property investor.

## PROFITING FROM INVESTMENT PROPERTIES

As I've touched on, owning an investment property has three distinct financial advantages: capital gain, income generation and tax savings. How you maximise these benefits will depend on the type of property you buy and your overall strategy.

### Capital gain

Perhaps you've heard the well-known saying that 'property doubles every seven years'. While such rhetoric should be taken with a grain of salt, history does show that real estate tends to appreciate over the long term.

If you own one home and its value increases significantly, you will likely then have sufficient equity to purchase a second property without needing to dip further into your personal savings. This is called 'leveraging' and it's a strategy used with great success by many real estate investors.

However, it's crucial to remember that the sword of leverage cuts both ways and in the event of a property market crash, you may experience amplified losses. This can be especially true where you have used equity in property A to purchase property B.

## Income generation

As well as capital appreciation, rental properties can provide a regular and direct financial return on your investment, usually on a weekly or monthly basis. This cash flow can serve as a reliable supplemental income or, for those with a substantial property portfolio, may even constitute their primary income source.

This rental revenue is typically adaptable over time. You have the flexibility to charge your tenants more or less in response to shifts in local economic conditions or changes in the cost of living (and after taking any rental agreements into account). This can assist in maintaining a steady income from your investment over an extended period.

Even in times of financial market turbulence, people still need places to live, which means property can often outperform other investment classes. However, it's important to factor in potential vacancies and the costs of ongoing maintenance and property management into your financial plans.

## Tax savings

The potential tax benefits of owning investment properties should not be overlooked. In a country like Australia, which is known for high taxation and complex tax legislation, owning an investment property can offer a legitimate and justifiable method of reducing your tax bill while simultaneously building your assets.

Over many years, this has proven particularly beneficial for employees, such as teachers, doctors and nurses, by helping them lower their tax burden and start accumulating wealth for their valuable contributions to society.

The extent of your tax benefits, however, will depend on how you 'gear' your property, which brings us to perhaps the most important section of this chapter!

# GEARING STRATEGIES

When you come to buy a property, you will need to carefully assess the relationship between the income generated and the expenses incurred. This will determine whether your investment will be positively or negatively geared, which, as I will now explain, is a crucial consideration.

## Negative gearing

Negative gearing is a fundamental concept in real estate investing and is particularly common in countries such as Australia. In simple terms, an investment is negatively geared when the expenses associated with owning a property, such as interest on the loan, property management fees, maintenance and depreciation, exceed the rental income generated.

At first glance, deliberately making a loss may seem counterintuitive to the principle of investing. However, an investor might choose a negatively geared property for strategic reasons.

The central tenet of negative gearing as an investment strategy is the belief in capital appreciation. Investors are willing to absorb short-term losses in return for expected long-term capital gains when the property's value increases. They bank on the future selling price being high enough to offset the operating losses and still provide a healthy profit.

Another crucial aspect of negative gearing lies in its tax implications. As I've mentioned already in this book, the loss from a negatively geared property can be offset against other income, reducing your taxable income and, therefore, your tax liability. This tax deductibility effectively provides a 'discount' on the cost of holding the property, making the net loss smaller than it would otherwise be.

For instance, someone who earns an annual income of $100,000 and makes a loss of $10,000 in a year on their investment property can reduce their taxable income to $90,000. Assuming that investor falls into a tax bracket of around 30 per cent, this reduction will result in tax savings of $3,000. So, in effect, the $10,000 loss only really costs the investor $7,000. The following table outlines this in more detail.

### Understanding the Numbers in Negative Gearing

| Description | Amount |
| --- | --- |
| Original annual income | $100,000 |
| Property's negative gearing loss | −$10,000 |
| Adjustable taxable income | $90,000 |
| Tax rate | 30% |
| Tax savings from negative gearing | $3,000 |
| Net loss after tax savings | $7,000 |

However, negative gearing is not without its risks. For one, it relies heavily on property values increasing over time. If the property market stagnates or declines, the investor may find themselves in possession of an asset that's valued at less than its purchase price. This could compound the continuous losses they've already incurred.

Additionally, negative gearing puts more pressure on an investor's cash flow since the rental income doesn't cover the property expenses – the need to find the shortfall from their other income. If they happen to lose their job or face unexpected expenses, they might find it difficult to maintain the property.

## Positive gearing

As you'd expect, positive gearing is the exact opposite of negative gearing. This occurs when the income produced by a property surpasses all costs related to its ownership and upkeep. Although this set-up might not immediately appeal to those in pursuit of tax deductions, the merit in possessing an asset that essentially pays for itself is undeniable.

This is particularly beneficial for investors looking for an additional and regular income stream. Positive cash flow can be used to cover personal expenses, pay down debt faster, save for future investments, or reinvest into the property itself to further increase its value.

As you approach retirement, it becomes increasingly important to consider the concept of positive gearing. While having a negatively geared property can bring tax benefits during your working years, when you're earning less income, you will want to minimise any ongoing debt service payments.

To transition your property portfolio from negatively geared to positively geared, you may need to reduce your mortgage debt, which can be achieved by reinvesting any surplus cash back into mortgage on the property.

## TYPES OF INVESTMENT PROPERTIES

So far in this chapter, I have spoken very broadly about investment properties, but now it's time to delve deeper into the specifics. Each type of investment property brings its unique set of characteristics and potential returns to the table. Let's examine the pros and cons of each to help you decide which may be right for you.

## Existing dwellings

An existing dwelling refers to any residential property that is not newly constructed, including houses, apartments and townhouses. These generally prove lucrative – particularly if they're located in an in-demand area.

Generally, investing in this type of property can be as easy as acquiring the property, finding tenants and sitting back as the rental income starts to flow. You barely have to give it a second thought, aside from taking care of the necessary maintenance that comes with older properties.

However, it's important to note that while the process of investing in established dwellings can be simpler, it might not offer the same tax benefits as purchasing a new property.

## 'Off-the-plan' properties

Off-the-plan properties are properties purchased before they are built, based on the blueprint provided by the developer. This option provides investors with the opportunity to secure a property at today's prices, potentially reaping the benefits of capital growth during the construction period.

While investing off-the-plan does have its advocates, I'm somewhat sceptical of it, as are many other property experts. The reasons for this scepticism are primarily tied to the unpredictable nature of real estate markets. In some instances, property prices have risen during the construction phase and developers have cancelled contracts, returned deposits and instead sold the properties at their new higher values, leaving the initial investor out of the deal.

Unfortunately, when prices move in the other direction, investors can also be stung because their contract will usually hold them to the agreed price. So, if you've committed to a $900,000 settlement but the property's value has dropped to $650,000, you're still on the hook for the full amount. In addition, supply chain issues in the post-pandemic world mean that construction costs and timelines have the ability to blow out considerably. This has meant the industry is far from stable. Along with a swag of construction company collapses, off-the-plan builds also involve more significant risks.

## New builds

Newly built properties, like off-the-plan properties, offer investors a brand-new property, but in this case are already constructed at the time of purchase. They often come with builder warranties, modern designs and energy-efficient features, attracting a high calibre of tenants.

Another notable advantage for investors of a new build over an older property is the tax benefits. New builds come with a higher proportion of depreciable assets, which can lead to substantial deductions. New appliances, carpets and even structural elements can be depreciated over time. (Your accountant can provide further advice in this area.)

With a new build, you also benefit from a builder's warranty, offering some peace of mind because it covers defects and issues that may arise during a specified period post-construction. This level of protection is not available when purchasing an older, estab-lished dwelling. Note that this may not apply for high rise property.

However, as with any investment option, you also have intricacies and potential drawbacks to consider. New builds are often situated in a newly developed area, which can mean limited amenities, a less stable property market and a larger supply of property for rent.

## House and land

Unlike off-the-plan properties or new builds, a house and land package involves buying a vacant plot of land and then contracting a builder to construct a new home on that land. This can present an affordable entry point for many investors, particularly in suburban or rural areas that are situated further out from more expensive inner-city locations.

However, it's again worth noting that if you build a house in these further-out areas, it can be harder to find tenants and long-term capital gains may not be as attractive.

## Commercial properties

Commercial properties include office spaces or buildings leased to businesses. These properties offer long-term lease agreements, often over several years, resulting in a stable, long-term income stream. However, they can be more susceptible to economic down-turns, which can affect the tenants' ability to pay rent.

## Industrial properties

Industrial properties encompass spaces such as warehouses and factories. These investments often deliver higher returns compared to residential or commercial properties. However, they require a larger initial investment and can also be sensitive to economic cycles.

## Real estate investment trusts (REITs)

For investors looking for exposure to real estate without the need to buy and manage properties, real estate investment trusts (REITs) can be an excellent choice. They allow investors to buy shares in companies that own and operate income-generating real estate. However, keep in mind you will have no direct control over the properties and need to rely on the management skills of the REIT.

## RENOVATIONS

Buying an investment property with a plan to renovate can be attractive because it comes with the possibility of adding substantial value. However, the process of trying to transform a rundown place into an attractive asset comes with inherent complexities and potential pitfalls.

Firstly, it's critical to remember that the property will be vacant during the renovation process, meaning you won't have a tenant helping you service your loan. Each and every repayment, along with the renovation costs, will be entirely on you.

Renovations almost always cost more than you expect as, unlike an entirely new build, they often involve unforeseen complications. Hidden issues such as outdated wiring, plumbing defects or structural weaknesses might not become apparent until work is underway, potentially adding significantly to the project's cost.

Then there are the costs of development applications and the challenge of finding a builder who understands the nuances of such projects. That's, of course, unless you try to do the job yourself, in which case you have to ask yourself: how much time can you dedicate to the project? Do you have a contingency plan for inevitable delays? And what are the financial implications?

My wife and I once considered a renovation project on an old church. While the potential was exciting, the reality of the financial cost and the complexity of marrying the new with the old meant we had to put aside our emotions and pass on the opportunity.

Renovation projects are generally not a quick means to make money. They require specific skills, significant financial resources and an expectation of delayed timelines. It's not for everyone and certainly not for beginners in property investment. So, proceed with caution in this realm.

# LESSON BLOCK: KEY CONSIDERATIONS OF PROPERTY INVESTMENT

Purchasing an investment property can be a very smart move for your long-term financial future, but before you take the plunge ensure you have considered the following:

- *Property structuring:* It is critical to get professional advice on structuring your property investment. There are potential tax advantages you may not even be aware of. (See chapter 21 for more on investment structuring.)
- *Your team:* Surround yourself with a team of experts in various fields, including accounting, law and financial coaching. The team should also include specialists relevant to your investment strategy, such as a reputable letting agent. Choosing the right people is vital to successful property management.
- *Local regulations:* While investing interstate can open up new opportunities, differences in regulations can pose challenges. Some states impose heavier land tax burdens on investors as well as potential rent caps, underlining the importance of seeking advice from your accountant and letting agent.
- *Choice of letting agent:* Having a trusted letting agent to select suitable tenants and conduct regular property inspections is crucial. You want to ensure your property is well maintained and any damage is promptly addressed.
- *Depreciation reports:* A depreciation report is essential, especially for new builds, because it outlines what you can claim for tax purposes. This report should be updated annually for the most accurate results.
- *Insurance coverage:* Landlord insurance is an essential component of property investment, providing coverage for various scenarios including vacancy periods, damage or potential litigation against a tenant.
- *Fire safety measures:* Regular checks and servicing of smoke detectors and other fire safety equipment is a legal requirement and should be on your checklist as a landlord.

- *Loan refinancing:* Refinancing can provide you with the equity needed to buy another property, and also potentially secure a better interest rate. It's important to strike a balance to avoid over-gearing, which could leave you in a vulnerable financial position.

Small adjustments such as getting a better insurance policy, a slightly better finance rate or improved depreciation schedule might seem minute, but they can significantly affect your bottom line, especially as your property portfolio grows.

## GET STARTED!

Once you've completed your due diligence and have a clear understanding of the type of property that fits your investment strategy, proceed with finding an investment. Investigate potential areas and properties. Look at historical price growth, rental yields, vacancy rates, future development plans in the area and any other factors that could affect property value and rental income.

Be prepared for potential challenges such as market fluctuations and tenant-related issues. Monitor your investment regularly and make adjustments as necessary based on market trends and changes in your financial situation.

## 5-POINT ACTION PLAN

1. Determine whether your investment approach leans more towards negative or positive gearing. Would you prefer an investment property that provides tax benefits and potential for capital appreciation (negative gearing) or one that generates positive cash flow (positive gearing)?

2. Familiarise yourself with the types of investment properties available: existing dwellings, off-the-plan properties, new builds, house and land, commercial properties, industrial properties, and real estate investment trusts (REITs). Understand the unique characteristics, advantages and drawbacks of each type.

3. After acquiring a broad understanding of investment properties, it's time to seek expert advice tailored to your personal situation. Engage a proficient accountant and/or financial advisor to discuss potential tax benefits.

4. Research potential investment options, considering aspects such as historical price growth rental yields and vacancy rates.

5. As with any investment, monitor your investment property and aspects such as market fluctuations, tenant-related issues and your own financial situation. Make adjustments as required.

## ONLINE RESOURCES

Information on investment properties is almost as varied as the range of properties themselves. Visit wealthplaybook.com.au to understand our philosophy and decision making for investing in property today.

# Part IV

# MONEY MANAGEMENT

# Chapter 20

# DYNAMICS OF PLANNING

A man who does not plan long ahead will find trouble at his door.
Confucius

By this stage of the book, it should be clear that lasting wealth is rarely built on the back of a few impulsive, high-stakes decisions. Instead, it's more often the result of consistently following a well-considered, long-term strategy.

In this chapter, I outline the factors to consider when devising such a strategy, taking into account not only the predictable events but also the potential for surprises. Life will always throw up unforeseen twists and turns, and having a plan to deal with them will help ensure your journey to financial freedom isn't derailed.

To use a corny analogy, your life plan should be attuned to the rhythm of your life and be flexible enough to adapt when that rhythm changes. If you're choreographing a dance, you will adjust your moves to always match the beat, and financial planning follows the same principle. You must anticipate opportunities and challenges in advance and know exactly how you'll respond to them.

Perhaps you have devised a life plan in the past, only for it to be unexpectedly disrupted by a family crisis or unexpected temptations. The reality is that life rarely follows our carefully crafted roadmaps, which is why we need to have back-up routes!

So, let's step through the process of creating resilient and adaptable plans that will help you grow and safeguard your wealth, regardless of any curve balls that come your way.

## PLANNING STAGES

The following figure outlines all that your financial strategy should cover and what it can provide.

**The Stages of a Good Financial Plan**

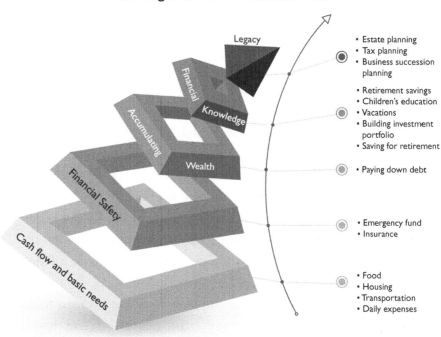

To establish an ironclad financial strategy, it's helpful to segment your life into six distinct stages: starting out, aggressive investing, accumulation, wealth explosion, pre-retirement and retirement.

Each stage brings its own unique set of circumstances and requires specific planning approaches to ensure success. Let's explore each stage in detail.

## Starting out phase (ideal age 10–20)

The 'starting out' phase is where you should begin to learn the basics of money management. Schools are only just starting to teach personal finance as a formal subject, so if you missed out you should take the initiative and educate yourself. Reading this book is a solid step to be taking! Most crucial is that you learn to be disciplined when it comes to budgeting and saving (as covered in chapter 3).

Another of the primary objectives during this phase is gaining employment. This could be a full-time job, or a part-time role if you're studying. Employment is not just about income; it's also a valuable experience that teaches you about work ethic, responsibility and the value of money.

During this stage, you should also be building an emergency fund (refer to chapter 8) and enough savings for a significant future investment. And while retirement may feel like a long way off, making early contributions to your superannuation fund can make a huge difference to your balance when the time comes.

In terms of risk profile, this phase leans aggressive. With time on your side, you can afford to take calculated risks to potentially reap higher returns. Appropriate asset classes for this phase include high-interest savings accounts, which offer a stable and risk-free return, growth stocks, which have a high potential for returns (albeit with increased risk), and ETFs, which provide a way to diversify while still targeting strong growth.

Setting clear, specific life and financial goals is also a fundamental objective during this phase. (Refer to chapter 2 for more on goal setting.) This is the time to reflect on what you want your future to look like and start plotting a course to get there. Your focus needs to be about more than numbers on a page. It's also about envisioning the life you want to lead and understanding how financial management can make that vision a reality.

### Aggressive investing phase (ideal age 20–30)

This phase generally kicks off when you complete your education, be it at school or university, and step into the workforce. Your initial focus for this period should be to manage any student loan debt, known as HECS-HELP debt in Australia, while continuing to focus on building an emergency fund and a healthy savings balance.

If you have a desire to enter the property market, you should plan to do that as early as possible. Initially, it may feel impossible to save the deposit and make the repayments, but by making sacrifices you can make it happen.

The earlier you acquire your first property, the more time you have to benefit from potential capital appreciation over the long term. From there, you can continue to accumulate wealth by purchasing rental properties and looking at other investments.

Personal milestones in the accumulation phase might include moving in with a partner, and perhaps even getting married and starting a family. These milestones come with their own financial implications and it's crucial to have open and honest conversations with your partner to develop a joint money plan that aligns your shared goals and values.

### Accumulation phase (ideal age 30–40)

The accumulation phase, typically spanning the ages of 30 to 40, is a pivotal period in your financial journey. At this stage, you are likely to be earning a more substantial income than you were in your twenties and have a golden opportunity to significantly accelerate your wealth-building efforts.

During the accumulation phase, you should look to aggressively grow investment portfolios. This could encompass a variety of strategies, such as diversifying across different asset classes like stocks, bonds and real estate, or even starting a side hustle to generate additional income streams. It is a time marked by active engagement in investments, with property, stocks and ETFs being especially relevant asset classes, aligning with a risk profile that is moderate to aggressive.

One key aspect of this phase is the prioritisation of paying off high-interest debts. This will enable you to then redirect substantial resources towards wealth creation, effectively laying the groundwork for robust financial health in later years.

Another key objective during this phase might be considering the transition to a self-managed super fund (SMSF), possibly in conjunction with a partner, to have greater control over retirement savings. It is also a time to carefully factor in new expenses, such as those associated with starting (or growing) a family. As rental income begins to accumulate, purchasing additional investment properties may become a viable and attractive option.

## Wealth explosion phase (ideal age 40–50)

The wealth explosion phase ideally happens between the ages of 40 and 50. During this pivotal decade, the power of compounding truly starts to take effect, leading to a substantial increase in personal wealth.

People in this stage often begin to refine their portfolios, managing risk effectively through a balanced mix of moderate to aggressive investments, including property, stocks, ETFs and a small percentage of high-growth 'exotic' investments.

Tax-efficient strategies become a focal point, prompting considerations for changes to investment structures to ensure maximum benefits. It is also a time for individuals to review and rebalance their portfolios regularly, ensuring alignment with their evolving financial goals and risk tolerance.

Securing maximum income insurance during this phase is crucial, with this serving as a safeguard for your growing wealth and solidifying financial stability for the forthcoming retirement years.

## Pre-retirement phase (ideal age 50–60)

The pre-retirement phase is where you make the transition from accumulating investments to using these assets as the primary source of income. As this phase commences, it becomes essential to clearly define what you envision your ideal retirement to be.

This involves mapping out lifestyle choices, identifying your needs and expectations, and deciding the optimal age to retire, which could be 55, 60, or beyond. These decisions are pivotal, because they directly influence the financial strategy that will support your desired retirement lifestyle.

Amid continued changes to government legislation, shifting retirement age thresholds, and escalating living costs, the challenge of retirement planning can intensify. For this reason, engaging with a trusted advisor becomes crucial, because they can analyse potential risks and devise strategic plans for a smooth transition into retirement.

Importantly, these discussions should be holistic, addressing not only the financial components of retirement but also the emotional and mental adjustments that accompany the transition from a long standing career, which may have greatly shaped your identity.

In the pre-retirement phase, the emphasis is on retiring debt – a fundamental step towards a comfortable, stress-free retirement. For instance, a 55 year old with several investment properties might contemplate selling a portion of them.

This phase sees a strategic move away from negative gearing towards establishing a positive income flow. Your risk profile during this phase becomes more conservative, with suitable asset classes often including dividend-paying stocks, property and ETFs.

## Retirement phase (ideal age 60+)

For those who have built a substantial nest egg, the retirement phase should be a time of relaxation and enjoyment, reaping the fruits of years of labour and prudent financial management.

With people living longer due to improved health and wellbeing factors, ensuring that your savings can sustain this extended period is critical. This longer life expectancy also correlates with potentially higher healthcare costs in retirement. As such, you should secure appropriate health insurance coverage or allocate a portion of savings for potential medical expenses.

Effective investment portfolio management remains important in the retirement phase. Retirees must strike a balance between investing in relatively safe financial instruments that yield steady income and those offering higher returns but at increased risk.

In this phase, key objectives include returning to strict budgeting and regularly reviewing estate plans, ensuring that wills, trusts and beneficiary designations remain current. Additionally, it may make sense to reduce life insurance and income protection expenses.

Appropriate asset classes during retirement often encompass dividend-paying stocks, property and ETFs. These investments are designed to provide a steady, reliable income stream, aligning with the overarching goal of this phase: to secure a comfortable and financially stable lifestyle while vigilantly managing a now-fixed income.

## EXTERNAL SHOCKS

In the introduction to this chapter, I mentioned how the best laid plans can be thrown into disarray because of unforeseen twists and turns – what I call 'external shocks'. These are unexpected events that can pose challenges at any stage of your life. Some of the surprises you should factor into your planning are outlined in the following sections.

### Divorce

Statistics show that approximately 50 per cent of marriages and de facto relationships in Australia break down. This makes it absolutely imperative that you factor the possibility of your marriage or relationship ending into your financial plan – as difficult as that thought can be.

Divorce and relationship breakdown is a significant life event that can have profound financial implications. The division of assets can have a substantial impact on both parties involved. This is why it's essential to approach your contingency plan with careful consideration and potentially seek professional advice.

Creating a prenuptial or postnuptial agreement can help establish clear guidelines for asset division. While it may seem unromantic, these agreements provide a level of financial security and protection for both parties, ensuring a smoother transition if the relationship ends.

## Inheritance

Not all 'external shocks' in your financial life will be negative. In the sad event of a family member passing away, you may find yourself inheriting a large amount of money. For example, being left a house these days could add millions of dollars to your net worth overnight.

While it may be tempting to sell any assets and spend the money on luxury items such as cars, boats and holidays, you should instead give careful consideration to how you handle the windfall. Rather than viewing it as a one-time infusion of cash for immediate gratification, you should think about how it can be transformed into a substantial asset that delivers consistent income for the rest of your life.

It is worth noting that the rules and regulations surrounding inheritance vary from country to country. In the United Kingdom, for example, considerations such as inheritance tax require careful navigation.

When integrating an inheritance into your financial plan, it is essential to have open and transparent communication with your family members and loved ones involved. This ensures a shared understanding among all, and that the legacy is employed in a fashion that resonates with your family's collective aspirations and principles.

## Litigation

Facing litigation can be a highly challenging and disruptive event in your financial journey. Whether you find yourself embroiled in a lawsuit or facing the possibility of being sued, it is crucial to be prepared and have appropriate risk management strategies in place.

Legal fees can quickly accumulate, and without proper insurance coverage, you may find yourself having to tap into your property or other assets to fund your defence. This can significantly impact your financial stability and force you to make difficult decisions.

One essential risk management tool to consider is Directors and Officers Liability Insurance, which provides coverage for legal expenses in cases where company directors and officers are facing claims. (This relates to how your investments are structured, which I cover in the next chapter.)

Regardless of your business structure or situation, it is crucial to seek expert legal advice and guidance. A skilled lawyer specialising in the relevant area of law can provide valuable insights and strategies to navigate through the legal process. They can help you understand your rights, responsibilities and potential outcomes, allowing you to make informed decisions.

In high-risk professions or situations, the potential for legal action is a genuine concern. In the next chapter, I explain how to take proactive steps to protect your assets by holding them outside of your personal name.

## Injury or illness

Another significant challenge that can derail financial plans is an unexpected injury or disability.

In chapter 23, I outline why having adequate insurance coverage, such as total permanent disability (TPD) or income protection insurance, should be factored into your planning. These policies can provide a financial safety net by replacing lost income or providing compensation for disability-related expenses.

Failing to have the appropriate insurance coverage in place can create a significant external shock, as you suddenly find yourself out of the accumulation phase and thrust into the immediate drawdown phase, relying solely on your existing assets for income.


## Market crashes

Market crashes can have a profound impact on your financial plans and it's important to recognise that they are not always within your control. Countless stories emerged of people who'd retired weeks before the global financial crisis (GFC) hit and suddenly found their investment portfolio had dropped 40 per cent in value.

The GFC is an extreme example, but even watching your asset pool shrink 15 per cent – from, for example, $1,000,000 to $850,000 – would come as a shock. The $150,000 deficit could considerably impact your retirement income and lifestyle.

Similar risks are also present if you're invested in the property market. For example, if you'd been benefiting from considerable returns through commercial property investment prior to the pandemic, you may have been shocked by skyrocketing vacancy rates as an increasing number of people worked from home and businesses downsized their corporate office spaces.

This is why it is always important to have a diversified portfolio and to ensure your financial plan remains fluid and adaptable, ready to respond to the ever-changing economic landscape. It must retain this dynamic characteristic throughout its duration, from the moment you formulate it until the time comes to execute your will.

## SEEK ADVICE

Seeking advice from a professional is a smart move when planning something as important as your financial future. While books and podcasts can provide valuable insights and knowledge, the dynamic nature of financial planning necessitates personalised guidance that considers your specific circumstances. A trusted advisor can help you adapt your plan as your life evolves, helping to ensure unexpected events become mere blips on your journey rather than overwhelming craters.

Engaging in regular conversations with an advisor allows you to address the ever-changing threads of your life. As you experience new milestones, challenges and opportunities, your advisor can provide tailored recommendations and strategies to keep you on track toward your financial goals. They can help you make informed decisions, sidestepping potential pitfalls and maximising opportunities. (Refer to chapter 6 for more on building your team of trusted advisors.)

## REFER TO THE 'PLAYBOOK'

In the final part of this book, I provide you with a 'playbook' that summarises each phase of the financial journey and clearly defines the actions you should be taking during each phase. This playbook is designed to serve as a handy reference guide that you can keep within arm's reach and refer to continually when needed.

## 5-POINT ACTION PLAN

1. Start planning for retirement as early as possible. Be flexible and adapt your retirement goals to cope with changing personal circumstances, as well as evolving economic and legislative scenarios.

2. Recognise and plan for the starting out, aggressive investing, accumulation, wealth explosion, pre-retirement and retirement phases of your financial life. Develop detailed financial strategies that cater to each phase's unique requirements.

3. Prepare for potential external shocks, such as divorce, inheritance, litigation, severe illness or market crashes. Build contingency plans and employ risk management strategies to maintain financial stability during these challenges.

4. Allocate time and resources towards seeking advice and enhancing your financial literacy. By doing so, you'll be equipping yourself with the knowledge required to make strategic and well-informed decisions, thereby strengthening your overall financial planning process.

5. Refer to the playbook provided in the final part of the book, which clearly defines the actions you should be taking during each phase of your life. Keep it accessible and review it regularly to ensure you are staying on track with your financial goals.

## ONLINE RESOURCES

The dynamics of good planning is a constantly shifting environment. Events change as do your circumstances. To keep you on track, regular workshops on the dynamics of investing are available at wealthplaybook.com.au.

# Chapter 21

# YOUR INVESTING STRUCTURE

It's not just what you own; it's how you own it.

Andrew Baxter

Novice investors are usually very keen to talk about exciting topics such as which assets to buy and when to buy them, but few pay enough consideration to the type of legal entity that will be making the purchase. This approach is similar to being caught up in the thrill of planning a road trip and giving no thought to the car you'll be driving. Sure, the destination is important, but so is the vehicle that gets you there.

So, in this chapter, it's time to look at your investing structure, which essentially refers to the legal framework under which your investments are held. It may sound like a mundane topic, but the implications for your financial journey can be significant. Get it right, and you'll see significant long-term benefits. Get it wrong, and you'll be on the road to disaster.

Incorrect structuring could lead to an unnecessary tax burden, increased risk exposure and complexities in transferring ownership. In contrast, an optimal investment structure can provide tax efficiency and a high level of asset protection.

# TYPES OF INVESTMENT STRUCTURES

Before you take the plunge into acquiring assets, it's important to carefully assess the range of investment structure options available and choose the one that aligns most closely with your needs. A universal 'perfect' structure doesn't exist, because every investor's circumstances are unique and demand a personalised approach.

To kickstart the decision-making process, the following sections examine the pros and cons of the four principal types of investment structures.

## Individuals

When starting out, investing in your own name is undeniably the most straightforward path to take. Whether you're dabbling in the stock market via a brokerage account or making a more substantial commitment, such as buying your first home, this approach can be perfectly adequate.

A significant advantage of investing under your own name is the freedom to oversee your assets as you see fit. This autonomy applies to both the gains and losses incurred from your investments, which directly affect you and instantly influence your personal tax obligations.

Additionally, investing in your own name keeps administration simple. You're not required to prepare separate tax returns or provide balance sheets that would otherwise be necessary with more complex investment structures. This simplicity allows you to focus on the essential task of managing your investments without getting tangled in a web of paperwork.

However, investing as an individual is not without its downsides. The big one is the risk of personal liability. In a worst-case scenario, should an investment default or be subjected to a lawsuit, your personal assets – including your home or savings – could be at risk.

What's more, the tax implications of individual investing could prove unfavourable. If your investments nudge you into a higher income tax bracket, the resulting taxes on your investment gains could significantly diminish your returns.

## Partnerships

A partnership, or joint investment structure, typically refers to two or more people sharing ownership of an investment. This is common among married couples, business partners or even friends.

Partnership-based investments offer the unique opportunity to pool resources together, potentially giving the participants access to larger or more diverse investment opportunities than they might be able to afford individually.

This structure also helps distribute risk among the parties involved. Each member shares the potential losses, which can lessen the financial blow should the investment not perform as expected. Usually, responsibilities and profits in a joint venture are divided proportionally among the co-investors, making the process equitable and balanced.

However, be aware that investing as a partnership opens the door to disagreements, conflicts and legal disputes among the parties. Decision-making can become a challenge if individuals aren't on the same page. This can cause operational difficulties and, in worst-case scenarios, affect the performance of the investment itself.

It is also crucial to note that typically, each co-owner is legally accountable for actions executed under the banner of the joint investment. This means that any legal or financial consequences resulting from the investment will be shouldered by all partners, adding another layer of potential risk.

For these reasons, it's essential to lay a solid foundation from the beginning with clear and formal agreements outlining each partner's responsibilities, the division of profits and losses, and procedures for dispute resolution. While this may seem overly cautious at the onset, it can prevent a multitude of issues down the line, ensuring the partnership remains both profitable and harmonious.

## Companies

In this structure, the company acts as a separate legal entity that owns the investment assets and the investors become the shareholders of the company. A key advantage of investing via a company structure lies in the limited liability it offers.

In simple terms, this means that if the company incurs debt or faces a lawsuit, the shareholders' personal assets are typically shielded from any legal or financial fallout. This level of protection can provide investors with the peace of mind to venture into riskier investments, knowing that their personal wealth is safeguarded.

Further to this, the company structure can yield potential tax benefits. Often, corporate tax rates are lower than personal tax rates, which could mean more of your returns stay in your pocket instead of going to the taxman.

Beyond the financial benefits, a company structure can also enhance the professional perception of the investor in the eyes of clients and partners. This credibility can potentially lead to more significant investment opportunities and business relationships.

However, you must also consider the administrative responsibilities associated with managing a company. This structure requires more work in terms of record keeping, maintaining special bank accounts, filing separate tax returns and holding regular company meetings. These obligations can increase the complexity of managing your investments and may require additional resources or professional help.

Another important consideration is the possibility of double taxation. While the company may enjoy lower tax rates, profits distributed to shareholders as dividends might be further taxed if the individual is on a higher marginal tax rate. This is known as 'top up tax' and could potentially erode your net return on investment, depending on your specific tax situation. Hence, by being correctly structured, you should be unaffected by this.

## Trusts

A trust is a distinct investment structure that allows a third party, known as the trustee, to hold and manage assets on behalf of one or more beneficiaries. Trusts can be customised to a great extent, allowing for detailed specifications on how and when the assets are to be transferred to the beneficiaries.

One of the significant advantages of trusts is the enhanced level of asset protection they offer. By placing assets into a trust, they are generally shielded from potential personal liabilities, providing a protective layer for your investments. Trusts can also yield potential tax benefits, making them an attractive option for high net-worth individuals or families.

However, setting up and managing a trust does come with associated challenges. Trusts can be complex to establish, often requiring comprehensive legal and financial advice to ensure they are correctly set up and administered. Furthermore, they require a higher standard of accounting practices to maintain transparency and fulfil legal requirements.

Alongside the complexities, you also need to consider the cost implications. Due to the legal and administrative intricacies, trusts can be expensive to establish and maintain. As a result, this investment structure might not be suitable for everyone, especially those with simpler financial situations or smaller portfolios.

The table on the following page outlines the four main types of trusts, providing an overview of their functions, benefits and potential drawbacks.

### Types of Trust Structures

| | |
|---|---|
| **Discretionary trusts** | Often referred to as family trusts, discretionary trusts give the trustee the ability to determine the allocation of trust income or capital among beneficiaries. This flexibility paves the way for strategic income distribution among trust members, which can result in substantial tax benefits by effectively lowering the overall tax liability. This could be especially advantageous when beneficiaries fall under different tax brackets. (However, keep in mind strict anti-avoidance provisions are in place in Australia to discourage trustees from distributing unearned income to children under the age of 18.) |
| **Unit trusts** | Unit trusts are rigid in their structure. In a unit trust, the trust property is divided into units, similar to shares in a company. Each unit gives the holder a proportional beneficial interest in the trust property. These trusts are commonly used for joint ventures and managed investment schemes due to their transparency and simplicity compared to discretionary trusts. |
| **Testamentary trusts** | A testamentary trust is a trust created by a will. It comes into effect upon the death of the person who made the will. These trusts can be beneficial for providing for minors and ensuring assets are distributed in accordance with the will as well as protecting assets and offering potential tax efficiency. |
| **Bloodline trusts** | Bloodline trusts, sometimes called 'generation-skipping trusts', are designed to keep assets within a particular family bloodline. They provide for children, grandchildren and subsequent generations, and protect the assets from claims by spouses or ex-spouses. Bloodline trusts can be an effective tool for asset protection and estate planning, but they are complex and should be established with legal and financial advice. |

## Superannuation

I talk more about superannuation in the next chapter, but it can also make sense to invest through a self-managed super fund (SMSF). An SMSF is a private superannuation fund that you manage yourself.

It can offer significant control over your retirement savings, along with the flexibility to invest in a wide range of assets. However, with increased control comes increased responsibility and regulatory oversight.

In the following chapter, I delve into the specifics of SMSFs, including their advantages and potential challenges, and whether they might be a suitable choice for your investment needs.

## CASE STUDY: STRUCTURING EXPENSES FOR OPTIMAL TAX BENEFITS

You may be aware that the costs incurred by the ownership of a car in your business name can present opportunities for tax benefits. When a vehicle is used for business purposes, expenses related to its operation and maintenance may be tax-deductible. This includes fuel, insurance, repairs and even depreciation.

However, the possibilities don't end there. I know a couple who took it a step further by purchasing a yacht that would be used partly for personal recreation. Through their business, they cleverly acquired naming rights to the boat as a marketing expense, which was tax-deductible.

By securing the naming rights and adorning the boat with their company's name and logo, the yacht transformed into a floating advertisement for their business. This served as a remarkable platform for showcasing their brand, capturing attention and increasing its visibility and reach.

It's important to note that for this strategy to remain valid, the boat must predominantly serve business purposes. The couple would need to work out the proportion of time the yacht was used for business purposes (versus personal recreation purposes) and only claim this same proportion of expenses. Keeping detailed records, potentially including a logbook, is crucial to substantiate your claims if ever questioned by tax authorities.

> Therefore, although this strategy appears clever, it requires careful consideration and professional guidance to determine its applicability to your unique situation and ensure compliance with prevailing tax laws.

## CHOOSING THE RIGHT STRUCTURE FOR YOU

The following table summarises the possible advantages and disadvantages of each investment structure covered in this chapter.

**The Right Structure For You**

| Structure | Advantages | Disadvantages |
| --- | --- | --- |
| Individual/in your own name | Easiest place to start | Maybe less tax efficient<br>Offers no asset protection |
| Company | Potentially lower tax<br>Some asset protection | Admin costs<br>Assets are not fully protected |
| Discretionary trust | Asset protection<br>Tax effectiveness<br>Estate planning | Admin costs<br>Only profits, not losses can be distributed<br>May be more difficult to borrow for property purchase |
| Self-managed superannuation fund | Lowest tax environment<br>Excellent asset protection<br>Intergenerational planning | Admin costs<br>Responsibilities as trustee<br>Access to funds limited by age |

As I've highlighted in this chapter, you need to consider numerous factors when choosing the most appropriate investing structure for your needs.

Ultimately, the right decision is dependent on your circumstances, which can change with time! Significant life events such as marriage, divorce and career shifts can serve as triggers for a structural re-evaluation. You also need to keep abreast of any tax law changes or developments in economic conditions that could have an impact on the type of investment structure you've chosen,

To ensure you find the optimal fit for you, it will pay to seek the help of a professional who can provide personalised advice based on your financial goals and evolving situation.

## 5-POINT ACTION PLAN

1. Start by gaining a firm understanding of the different investment structures – individuals, partnerships, companies and trusts – and how each can influence your financial journey. Appreciate the significance of the structure you choose and how it can impact your tax liabilities, asset protection and investment flexibility.
2. Undertake a comprehensive review of your personal circumstances. Your current financial standing, future goals, and potential life changes should all factor into your decision-making process.
3. Reassess your chosen structure, particularly when significant life events occur. Changes such as marriage, divorce or career shifts can necessitate structural adjustments to optimise your investment strategy.
4. Stay informed about changes in tax laws, economic conditions or any other factors that could influence the effectiveness of your chosen structure. Constant education will empower you to make proactive adjustments and optimise your investment strategy over time.

5. To ensure you are making an informed decision, engage the services of a professional who can provide personalised advice based on your specific needs and help navigate the complexities of investment structures.

## ONLINE RESOURCES

Check out the online Success Portal at wealthplaybook.com.au for more on investing structure.

# Chapter 22

# SUPERANNUATION

You can be young without money,
but you can't be old without it.
Tennessee Williams

If you're a single person in your twenties, the topic of superannuation probably sounds boring and somewhat irrelevant. You might feel you have more pressing financial matters to deal with than planning for your retirement. However, as you become older, it's likely your superannuation will become a bit of a fixation. And you'll wish you'd started thinking about it sooner.

Indeed, in Australia, the superannuation system serves as the cornerstone for a financially secure post-work life. After dedicating decades to your career, you deserve a period of leisure and personal enjoyment. Your retirement years shouldn't just be about survival, but should also be about relishing the fruits of your labour.

In this chapter, I run through the many different ways you can go about building your super balance, and help you find the best option for you.

## TYPES OF SUPER FUNDS

Two types of super funds are generally possible: 'defined contribution funds' (also known as accumulation funds) and 'defined benefit funds'. These days, most super funds are defined contribution funds, but it's still important to explain the difference.

### Defined contribution funds

In these funds, your final retirement benefit is not predetermined. Instead, it hinges on the contributions made over time and the performance of your fund's investments. The risk of investment is borne entirely by the individual, because the final payout will depend on market performance.

In Australia, it's a legal requirement that employers contribute a minimum percentage of an employee's earnings to a super fund. For the 2023–24 tax year, that amount is 11 per cent of your gross pay. (This will increase by 0.5 per cent each year until it reaches 12 per cent in the 2025–26 tax year.)

This money is usually added to your superannuation account on a weekly or monthly basis.

### Defined benefit funds

In these funds, you're guaranteed a certain percentage of your final salary upon retirement. My father-in-law, who was a teacher, was part of one of these funds and as a result enjoys a percentage of his final salary during his retirement years.

While these schemes can provide a degree of certainty for retirement, they aren't without their drawbacks. The income required to sustain payouts to thousands of beneficiaries derives from the scheme's asset pool and if the market underperforms, the asset pool's capital value must be used to meet income payouts.

This can negatively impact the scheme's younger or more recent members, leaving them at a disadvantage compared to older members who have been part of the scheme for a longer period.

## SUPER FUND CATEGORIES

When it comes to choosing where to park your retirement savings, it's imperative that you take the time to understand the distinct categories of super funds out there. Each category has its unique characteristics, benefits and potential pitfalls.

### Industry super funds

Industry super funds are typically established by industry bodies and trade unions for employees in specific industries, but most of them are now open to the general public. They operate on a not-for-profit basis, which means any earnings are returned to the fund to benefit its members.

These funds are managed by a board of trustees, with equal representation from employer associations and member (employee) representatives. This structure is designed to ensure a balanced approach in decision-making that focuses on the members' best interests.

In Australia, industry funds are an extremely popular choice for their ease of use, relatively low fees and solid performance. Most industry funds allow you to tailor the investment options your super-annuation is invested in – so you can choose between balanced, diversified, high-growth or sustainable options, for example.

However, each fund should be closely examined on its own merits, because some have come under scrutiny for their fee structures. There have also been cases of industry super funds being very slow on payouts, making significant donations to unions and recording poor performance.

## Retail super funds

Retail super funds, typically run by banks or investment companies, are another key category in the superannuation landscape. These funds are open to everyone and are popular because of the increased control, choice and flexibility they provide to investors.

Retail super funds usually offer even more options than industry super funds when it comes to tailoring your investments to suit your specific preferences. If you're an investor who thrives on the adrenaline of high stakes, you have the opportunity to opt for high-risk investment options, which, although risky, could potentially yield high rewards.

If you're a conservative investor seeking stability, they can offer you secure investments such as bonds and cash, which can provide steady, albeit lower, returns over time. Further, if you're environmentally conscious and value sustainable practices, retail super funds provide 'green' or socially responsible investment options.

However, with this increased flexibility and choice can also come higher fees. Retail super funds often have a fee-for-service structure, meaning you might pay for the additional features, investment options and services they provide.

Another potential downside of retail super funds is that they are typically profit-driven entities. These profits often go to shareholders, which could lead to a conflict of interest between maximising returns for fund members and providing profits for shareholders.

Also be aware that if you have a consultation with a financial planner, they might direct you to a retail super fund because they receive a financial benefit for doing so.

## Corporate super funds

Corporate super funds are generally established by large corporations, such as Australian airline Qantas, exclusively for their staff members. They often offer competitive fees and may have features specifically tailored to the employees of that company.

Such funds can prove very beneficial because they're often designed with the members' best interests in mind, offering attractive benefits such as insurance and financial planning services. The level of service and the benefits provided can be notably high in these funds, which is a big advantage for employees.

If you work for a company that offers a corporate super fund, it's well worth considering this as a viable option.

## Public sector super funds

Public sector super funds are tailored to meet the retirement needs of government employees. Although criticism often surrounds the generous benefits these funds offer politicians, it's important to recognise that they also serve a wide range of other government workers, including teachers, nurses, police officers and defence force personnel.

Public sector funds are known for their strong, consistent performance, security and relatively low fees. However, conditions and benefits can vary greatly depending on specific government policies.

## Self-managed super funds (SMSFs)

Self-managed super funds (SMSFs) are a unique and increasingly popular category of superannuation. As the name suggests, SMSFs provide the opportunity to take control of how your retirement savings are managed.

One of the key advantages of SMSFs is the level of control and flexibility they offer. Members act as trustees and have the autonomy to choose specific investments that align with their financial goals and risk tolerance.

One notable benefit is the ability to buy property within your super, which could prove to be a significant investment growth strategy. It's important to note, however, that all investments, including property, cannot be purchased for personal use. This is part of the 'sole purpose test', which ensures that the primary objective of the fund remains to provide retirement benefits to the members.

SMSFs can also provide tax advantages. As with all super funds, the tax rate on income from your SMSF investments is capped at 15 per cent, which is generally lower than personal income tax rates. This cap also applies to capital gains, but if the asset, such as an investment property, has been held for more than a year, the rate can reduce to 10 per cent. This can be another advantage of purchasing property from within a SMSF. In retirement, the income stream from an SMSF is tax free.

Another potentially helpful benefit of SMSFs is the ability to pool your money with up to five others, meaning you can combine the super balances of your family members. This is particularly helpful if you have a relatively low super balance, because forming an SMSF with less than around $250,000 is arguably not cost effective.

SMSFs can be extremely advantageous if you have the knowledge and time to manage them successfully; however, you should be aware they do come with risks and responsibilities.

Trustees are required to adhere to strict regulations and fulfil legal obligations, including maintaining accurate records, preparing financial statements and lodging annual tax returns. (Failure to meet these obligations can result in the tax office classifying the fund as 'non-complying', and its assessable incomes being taxed at the highest marginal tax rate.) Again, engaging the services of professionals is highly recommended to ensure compliance with regulatory requirements.

## KEY CONSIDERATIONS

When choosing the superannuation option that's right for you and your family, some key factors to consider include your appetite for risk and the insurances available through the fund.

## Risk appetite

Choosing the right super fund that aligns with your risk appetite is a critical aspect of retirement planning. Your risk appetite refers to how comfortable you are with the possibility of losing some or all of your investment in exchange for potential higher returns. Essentially, it's a balancing act between the level of risk you're willing to accept and the potential return you desire on your investments.

When determining your risk appetite, factors such as your financial goals, investment horizon and your personal comfort level with volatility play a role. If you are in your twenties or thirties, you may have a long-term investment horizon and, therefore, a higher capacity to recover from potential short-term losses. In this case, a super fund offering higher risk investment option might be more suitable. These options usually have a significant portion of their investments in assets such as shares or property, which have historically produced higher returns over the long term, despite their volatility in the short term.

On the other hand, if you're nearing retirement, preserving the wealth you've accumulated becomes crucial. You may not have the time to ride out market volatility and recover from substantial losses. As such, a lower risk super investment option, with a higher proportion of investments in stable assets such as bonds or cash, might be more appropriate.

However, opting for a low-risk super fund option doesn't necessarily mean your investment is entirely risk-free. While they may offer stability, these options could yield lower returns, potentially not keeping pace with inflation, which in turn risks reducing your purchasing power over time.

Remember, everyone's situation and risk tolerance is unique, so it's crucial to seek professional advice before making these decisions.

## Insurances

In the broader context of superannuation, a crucial aspect often overlooked is the component of insurance within super. A substantial number of people hold their life insurance and total and permanent disability (TPD) insurance within their superannuation funds, which gives them an efficient and convenient way to ensure financial security.

Life insurance provides a lump sum payment to your beneficiaries upon your death, helping them maintain their lifestyle in the unfortunate event of your passing. TPD insurance, on the other hand, offers a lump sum benefit if you become seriously disabled and are unable to work again.

By integrating these insurances within super, individuals often find it easier to manage premiums, because they are automatically deducted from the super balance, rather than out of pocket.

However, it's crucial to be aware of the potential ramifications of changes to your superannuation structure on these insurances. For example, in an effort to save costs, some people have moved towards self-managed super funds (SMSFs), often set up through online platforms. However, they have forgotten about their insurances when making this move.

Such inadvertent cancellation can have devastating consequences, leaving the investor and their families exposed to financial hardship in the event of death or permanent disability. Unfortunately, the discovery of such a lapse often happens when it's too late.

This is another reason why it's paramount to seek professional advice when making any changes to your superannuation arrangements. Experts can help you navigate the complex interplay between super and insurance, ensuring that your insurances remain intact and you're adequately protected. They can also help assess the appropriateness and adequacy of your current level of insurance cover, even if offered within your existing super fund, taking into account your personal circumstances and financial commitments.

## GET STARTED!

You'd be forgiven for feeling overwhelmed after reading about all of the super options out there but, as I always say, the most important thing you can do is make a start. You don't need to jump into a self-managed super fund straightaway – a retail or industry fund will certainly suffice early in your career. If you're already working, no doubt you have a super fund that your employer contributions are sent to. (If you've been working for a while, you might even have more than one.) Make sure you're happy with the fund you're with, based on your age, financial goals and comfort level with volatility. If the fund isn't right for you, changing or consolidating funds is a relatively easy process.

Then, as your life progresses, you might consider new strategies, such as pooling your resources with family! The key is to start where you are, gain an understanding of your current financial situation, and gradually refine your structure to align with your goals.

The journey towards a secure retirement isn't a sprint, but a marathon. Begin early, stay consistent, stay informed, and with these strategies, you can anticipate a retirement that's not just comfortable, but genuinely enjoyable.

## 5-POINT ACTION PLAN

1. Learn about the different types of super funds available and consider what suits your personal circumstances, risk tolerance and investment preferences.

2. As your life evolves, consider strategies such as pooling assets with family members via a self-managed super fund. Regularly review and update your plan to keep it aligned with your changing needs and objectives.

3. Determine how much risk you're willing to tolerate in your superannuation investment portfolio. Your age, financial goals and comfort level with volatility should inform this decision.

4. Consider the type and quality of the insurances offered by a super fund before signing up. Ensure you understand the implications of any changes to your super on these insurances, and seek professional advice if needed.

5. The most crucial step is to start taking an active interest in your superannuation. Check the fund you're already with and, if required, find a super fund more suited to your needs – and begin securing a comfortable and enjoyable retirement.

## ONLINE RESOURCES

To get the most from retirement takes effort, time and action. Access a powerful superannuation workshop at wealthplaybook.com.au.

# Chapter 23

# INSURANCE

A man who dies without adequate life insurance should
have to come back and see the mess he created.
Will Rogers

At the time of writing this book, my wife and I are blessed with five
children under the age of nine. In the years to come, the costs associated with their education, hobbies and daily needs are going to keep
adding up – there's no escaping it!

Thankfully, we have a level of income that can comfortably cover
these expenses, but what would happen if one of us were to die
unexpectedly? That's where life insurance comes in.

In this day and age, spending money to ensure your children have
a safety net in the unfortunate event of your passing is a necessary
evil. It is particularly important for parents of children who are still
many years away from being able to support themselves.

In this chapter, we're going to look at the key factors you should
consider before taking out life insurance, as well as the importance
of having separate coverage for instances where your ability to earn
an income is compromised.

# TYPES OF INSURANCE

As an investor, it's crucial to consider a diverse range of insurance options to safeguard your financial interests. This includes landlord insurance, professional indemnity insurance and directors insurance, which protect specific aspects of your investment portfolio.

However, the primary focus of this section is 'personal risk insurance', which can be classified into four distinct categories.

## Life insurance

Life insurance provides financial protection for your loved ones in the event of your death. The policy pays out a predetermined sum of money, known as the 'death benefit', to your beneficiaries. This can help cover various expenses, such as mortgage payments, outstanding debts, funeral costs and the ongoing financial needs of your family.

Life insurance ensures that your loved ones are not burdened with financial hardships during an already difficult time.

## Total permanent disability (TPD) insurance

TPD insurance offers coverage in the event that you suffer a total and permanent disability that prevents you from working or engaging in your chosen occupation. The policy provides a lump sum payment to help you adapt to your new circumstances and cover medical expenses, rehabilitation costs, ongoing care and any necessary modifications to your living environment.

TPD insurance provides crucial financial support, allowing you to maintain a decent quality of life despite the life-altering effects of a permanent disability.

## Income protection

Income protection insurance is designed to replace a portion of your income if you become unable to work for a period of time due to illness, injury or disability. This type of insurance provides a regular income stream, typically a percentage of your pre-disability earnings, during the period of your incapacity.

This insurance helps to ensure that you can meet your day-to-day living expenses, such as mortgage or rent payments, bills and other financial obligations, while you focus on your recovery and rehabilitation.

## Trauma insurance

Trauma insurance, also known as critical illness insurance, provides a lump sum payment if you are diagnosed with a specified critical illness or experience a traumatic event, such as a heart attack, stroke, cancer or major surgery.

The funds received can be used to cover medical expenses, seek specialised treatments, modify your living environment, pay off debts, or even take time off work to focus on recovery. Trauma insurance provides a financial safety net during times of significant health challenges, helping to ease the burden and allow you to concentrate on your wellbeing.

## HOW MUCH COVER DO YOU NEED?

The amount of insurance coverage you require will depend on your stage of life and personal circumstances. For example, if you have children in private school, you'll likely need more than someone who has kids in the public system. Similarly, a person with a large mortgage will need more than someone who has no debts.

In my business, I see clients with one of two main problems: they're under-insured or they're over-insured. Someone who is under-insured is usually underestimating how much money their family will need when they're gone. For example, $700,000 might sound like a lot of cover, but once a $500,000 mortgage is paid off, the family is then left with only $200,000 for all ongoing expenses. That won't last long.

At the opposite end of the spectrum are those who are covered for an amount that is far more than their family would need. While it may seem beneficial to have a substantial insurance payout, it's important to weigh that up against the size of the premiums you have to pay each year.

If you're someone who has a large policy because you once had large debts and multiple children at home, then you should reassess that coverage once the debts have been paid off and the kids have moved out.

This underlines the fluid nature of insurance coverage; it should evolve as your life circumstances change. That's why it's crucial to periodically review your financial status.

## CHOOSING A PROVIDER

When you are purchasing life insurance in Australia, providers are legally obliged to give you a product disclosure statement (PDS), which will provide the following key details:

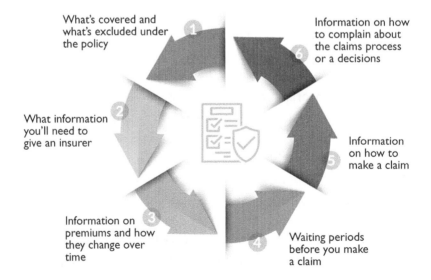

What's covered and what's excluded under the policy

What information you'll need to give an insurer

Information on premiums and how they change over time

Waiting periods before you make a claim

Information on how to make a claim

Information on how to complain about the claims process or a decisions

It's important to assess all of these factors, while also shopping around for the best price. Insurance companies are always keen to acquire new clients and increase their market share, meaning they'll usually offer attractive deals to convince you to sign up. Even if you can save $100 per month, it's worth the effort.

However, it is essential to ensure that you're always reading the fine print because cheaper quotes can come with reduced benefits. Policies will also come with a list of exclusions, which you should always read closely to ensure you'll be eligible for a claim. Some common exclusions include:

- *Suicide or self-harm:* Most life insurance plans have a suicide and self-harm clause that withholds benefits in claims involving suicide or attempted suicides if it occurs in the first 13 months of the policy.

- *Criminal activity:* Life insurance policies typically exclude claims related to criminal activity. If the insured person's death is a result of engaging in illegal activities or if they are found to have participated in criminal behaviour leading to their demise, the policy may not provide coverage.

- *Recklessness and negligence:* The recklessness and negligence exclusion pertains to injuries and deaths caused by the insured person's own reckless actions and personal negligence. Insurance companies may have their own criteria and varying levels of exclusions under this clause. Typically, it involves activities and incidents that any reasonable person would not take part in under normal circumstances.

- *Dangerous jobs:* Some life insurance policies may have limitations or exclusions for individuals working in high-risk occupations. If the insured person's death is a result of their occupation, such as military service or a hazardous profession, the policy may have specific provisions that limit or exclude coverage.

- *Risky hobbies:* Certain life insurance policies may include exclusions for deaths related to engaging in risky hobbies or extreme sports. If the insured individual's demise is a direct result of participating in activities deemed dangerous by the policy, such as skydiving or mountaineering, the coverage may not apply.

- *Pre-existing medical conditions:* While it is rare, some life insurance policies may include exclusions for ongoing medical conditions or illnesses that have a likelihood of recurring. It is important to review your insurer's policies to understand any specific limitations or exclusions related to your medical condition, because different insurers may have varying degrees of restrictions in place.

## CHECK YOUR SUPERANNUATION FUND

Before you make any decisions around life insurance, you should check whether you already have a policy through your super! Many super funds will automatically provide their members with a default level of cover that's typically calculated based on factors like your age and income. Check that the cover you're paying for is sufficient for your (and your family's) needs.

If you have multiple super funds, it may well be that you're paying for several life insurance policies, but if you were to die, you would likely only receive one payout. For this reason, make sure you cancel those you don't need.

If you have made a shift to a self-managed super fund, it's likely you inadvertently cancelled any policies you held in your previous super funds, so that is something to also keep in mind. In the event of your death, the last thing your family would need is finding out you had no cover.

## TAX DEDUCTIONS

According to the Australian Taxation Office (ATO), tax deductions can only be claimed for premiums paid to protect your income (salary and wages). However, a claim is not possible if the policy is held through a super fund and the premiums are deducted from your contributions.

Again, this highlights the importance of seeking professional advice on how to structure your affairs for optimal financial outcomes.

---

### 5-POINT ACTION PLAN

1. Evaluate your financial circumstances, including your current and future expenses, debts and dependents. Determine the amount of coverage required for each type of insurance.
2. Research and compare insurance providers. Compare their policies, benefits, exclusions and premium costs. Consider factors such as financial strength, customer reviews and claims processes to make an informed decision.
3. Carefully review the fine print and terms of each insurance policy. Pay attention to exclusions, waiting periods, claim processes and any limitations that may impact your coverage. Ensure that the policy aligns with your needs and offers the necessary protection.
4. Consult with a professional who can provide personalised guidance based on your individual circumstances.
5. Regularly review and update your coverage. Life circumstances change over time, so it's important to regularly review your insurance policies. As your financial situation evolves, reassess the adequacy of your coverage and make necessary adjustments.

## ONLINE RESOURCES

Keeping yourself up to date with your insurance needs can both provide peace of mind and save you money. For more information to assist you with your insurance, visit wealthplaybook.com.au.

# Chapter 24

# TIMES OF CRISIS

A crisis is a terrible thing to waste.

Paul Romer

If you stay in the investing game for long enough, you'll inevitably encounter periods of crisis. Already this century, we've experienced events such as the global financial crisis and the COVID-19 pandemic, which had seismic impacts on financial markets and tested the resilience of investors worldwide.

When such events occur, you can easily be overwhelmed by fear and panic. These reactions are understandable, given the potential risks and losses associated with market downturns.

However, history has shown that succumbing to hysteria can hinder our ability to make sound investment decisions. Over the years, I've witnessed firsthand the detrimental effects of failing to stay calm and keep a clear mindset.

In this chapter, I outline the strategies you can implement to weather the most violent of economic storms. I discuss how, with the right skills, it's possible to not just survive these events, but also profit from them!

## SURVIVING A CRISIS

Your first focus in the event of a crisis should be on safeguarding your existing capital. After all, you can only seize an opportunity to profit once your base capital is secure and protected.

How you respond will depend on which types of investments you have in your portfolio, so let's look at the main investment categories to formulate a tailored approach for each.

### Residential property

If you own multiple residential investment properties, a financial crisis can bring many challenges. You may encounter an abrupt fall in property values, face hurdles in securing new tenants, or deal with existing tenants who are unable to fulfil their rental obligations due to economic stress.

Generally, these situations will lead to one main problem for you as the landlord: an inability to extract enough cash flow from your properties to service the debt that is tied to them. If this happens to you, you can respond in several ways.

Firstly, you might consider refinancing your loans. This might involve negotiating a lower interest rate, extending the loan term, or switching from a variable to a fixed interest rate loan, all of which could potentially lower your monthly payments.

In some cases, a financial crisis may cause property values to fall but rental rates to increase. If market conditions are favourable and the demand for rental properties is high, you could also consider increasing the rent you charge your tenants. Your lease agreement will cover how often rent increases are allowed, and might provide a clause for a rent review, which lets you raise the rent proportionally to a Consumer Price Index (CPI) increase.

Another potential option is to reduce the amount of debt you have on the properties. This can be done by accessing any spare cash you have at your disposal, or by liquidating other investments.

## Commercial property

During a crisis, owning commercial real estate can pose unique challenges because they typically have higher vacancy rates during these times than residential properties. If you're finding it difficult to secure tenants, it may be beneficial to take proactive measures to enhance your property's appeal. This could involve offering temporary rent reductions or even rent-free periods to incentivise prospective tenants to commit to extended lease terms.

Securing long-term leases with dependable tenants can provide assurance to lenders and help to sustain the future income potential of your property. However, it's vital to carefully evaluate the impact of reduced rents on your property's valuation, given the direct correlation between property value and rental yield.

## Managed funds

If your investment portfolio includes a conventional managed fund, such as an Australian equities fund, and the market shows signs of significant downturn or potential recession, it might be wise to exit that investment.

Since these types of funds typically lack downside hedging strategies, they can be vulnerable to substantial losses. By exiting, you protect your capital and prevent further exposure to market downturns.

However, if your capital is invested in more flexible hedge funds, there may not be the same need to exit. These funds have the ability to modify their positions based on market shifts, meaning they can possibly take advantage of declines in the market.

## Direct shares

Deciding the optimal time to sell shares is inherently complex. However, if you possess the relevant skills, or have access to a competent team, it can be wise to review your share portfolio in a time of a crisis.

While it's true that markets typically bounce back over time, you can sometimes be left waiting for many years. And, in the meantime, you may miss out on significant investment opportunities that could have been leveraged had you safeguarded your capital initially.

During a crisis, it can often be wise to consider shifting from high-growth stocks to more defensive holdings such as utilities, pharmaceuticals or other resilient industries. If you have the necessary skill set, protective measures such as purchasing put options can also guard against downside risk while still keeping you engaged in the market.

## PROFITING FROM A CRISIS

At the start of this chapter, you will have seen the following quote: 'A crisis is a terrible thing to waste.' These words from Paul Romer, a renowned economist and Nobel laureate, recognise that periods of great uncertainty can also offer great opportunity.

With this in mind, let's now turn our attention to some of the ways you can attempt to profit from a crisis.

### Buying 'discounted' assets

During a crisis, the prices of shares, real estate and various other assets commonly experience significant declines. This downward pressure is often driven by market panic, investor sentiment and a general lack of confidence. While these price drops can be distressing for investors, they can also present unique opportunities for those who are prepared and have the means to capitalise on them.

One potential strategy is to adopt a contrarian approach, whereby you seek out undervalued assets that have the potential for long-term growth. By carefully analysing the fundamentals of a company or property and identifying those with strong underlying value, investors can take advantage of the market's irrational behaviour and acquire assets at discounted prices. However, it is important to conduct thorough due diligence and assess the risks associated with these investments.

## Investing in short ETFs

One strategy that can be employed during a crisis is investing in short exchange-traded funds (ETFs). Short ETFs are designed to profit from declining markets by taking short positions on specific indexes or sectors. These funds aim to generate returns that are inversely correlated to the performance of their underlying assets.

It is important to note that investing in short ETFs carries inherent risks. Market timing is crucial, and incorrectly predicting the duration or severity of a crisis can lead to losses. Further to that, short ETFs often employ leverage, which will amplify both gains and losses. Therefore, careful research, monitoring and risk management are essential when utilising this strategy.

## Investing in volatility

Volatility is a common characteristic of financial crises, presenting both challenges and opportunities for investors.

Investing in volatility can be achieved through various instruments, such as volatility index (VIX) futures, options or volatility-focused exchange-traded products. These instruments can be utilised to profit from extreme price swings.

---

### CASE STUDIES: TIMES OF CRISIS

With the benefit of hindsight, let's look at some of recent history's most significant crises and how investors could have used them to their advantage.

---

*Banking sector turmoil*

The most notable period of banking sector turmoil in recent history occurred during the global financial crisis. Some investors were able to profit from the chaos by short-selling individual banking stocks, or by carrying out short trades on financial sector ETFs.

Opportunities also existed to eventually take long positions on the bank stocks that had become undervalued during the crisis.

*Trade embargoes*

When China and Australia began a trade war in 2017, it was clear the impacts for investors would be significant, but it wasn't necessarily obvious which industries would suffer.

Australia's iron ore industry, for example, was relatively unaffected because China was too reliant on the raw material for its construction boom to impose tariffs or restrictions. However, a range of other sectors were not so fortunate, with China slapping heavy tariffs on wine, barley, lobsters, timber, red meat and cotton.

Astute investors will have reduced their exposure to companies in these sectors and potentially have taken short positions on some of them to capitalise on the unique situation.

*COVID-19 pandemic*

The COVID-19 pandemic brought about unprecedented challenges and disruptions across the global economy. However, amid the crisis, investors were able to identify opportunities and generate profits.

As well as investing in growth areas such as healthcare, biotech, e-commerce and digital entertainment, astute investors took short positions on companies affected by travel restrictions and lockdown measures, such as airlines, hotels and cruise lines.

*Rapid inflation*

Periods of rapid inflation pose unique challenges for investors, but there are ways to take advantage of the unique environment. During these times, bond yields tend to increase, causing bond prices to decline. In such situations, investments that profit from falling bond prices or rising yields can be advantageous. ETFs such as TBT in the US are designed specifically to perform inversely to the price of US Treasury Bonds, meaning they increase in value as bond prices fall.

Remember – short-selling individual stocks can be challenging, but other methods are also available, including the use of short ETFs, put options and futures contracts.

## BE ALERT

As you begin your investment journey, keep abreast of world events to ensure you are ready to respond to impact on markets. Substantial rewards are available for being agile and proactive. Importantly, you should never fear a crisis but instead be prepared with a strategic action plan and consider seeking advice when needed.

While it's important to be as self-reliant as possible, experienced professionals can provide valuable guidance during turbulent market conditions. Ultimately, it's not the crisis itself but your response to it that defines your investment success.

Having access to an advisory service during these times can be crucial.

## 5-POINT ACTION PLAN

1. Take a close look at your existing investment portfolio. Understand the different types of investments you have and how they might behave in a financial crisis.

2. Develop contingency plans for each type of investment in your portfolio. These plans should detail actions you might need to take in the event of a market downturn to safeguard your capital.

3. Understand and identify potential opportunities to profit during a crisis. This can include buying undervalued assets, investing in short ETFs and volatility trading. Research these investment avenues thoroughly to better understand associated risks and potential benefits.

4. Study historical cases of crises to understand how they unfolded and how investors responded. This will help you better grasp potential scenarios in the future and gauge the effectiveness of various strategies.

5. Don't hesitate to seek the advice of financial professionals. Experienced advisors can provide invaluable guidance when navigating turbulent market conditions. They can assist you in refining your contingency plans and help you identify profitable opportunities that align with your risk tolerance and investment goals.

## ONLINE RESOURCES

Check out the online Success Portal at wealthplaybook.com.au for more on managing times of crisis.

# Chapter 25

# MONEY MAINTENANCE

*The time to repair the roof is when the sun is shining.*
John F. Kennedy

Many things in life require regular maintenance: your house, your car, your health, your relationships and, similarly, your finances. Just like you wouldn't drive the family station wagon for 10 years without taking it for a service, you shouldn't assume your investments will take care of themselves forever.

Your goal should be to have your portfolio operating like a well-oiled machine, which means you need to constantly monitor its moving parts to ensure any issues are quickly identified and corrected. It's always better to perform regular upkeep rather than waiting for expensive repairs. As President John F. Kennedy told the United States Congress in 1962 (and as per the opening quote for this chapter), 'The time to repair the roof is when the sun is shining.'

Many people make the mistake of leaving their finances on autopilot and assuming everything will be okay. Sadly, when things inevitably go wrong, they can be very expensive to fix. For this reason, it's extremely important to have a maintenance plan.

In this chapter, I provide a practical timetable for the check-ups you should be carrying out on an annual, quarterly and monthly basis.

## ANNUAL MAINTENANCE

Whether it's at the end of the financial year, or the end of the calendar year, you should make time for a comprehensive annual review of your financial situation. This will help set you up for another successful 12 months ahead. Some key items that should be on your annual maintenance checklist are covered in the following sections.

### Life insurance

As discussed in chapter 23, your level of life insurance coverage should be regularly assessed to ensure it remains appropriate for your current needs. Questions you should ask yourself include:

01 Have you accumulated more debt?

02 Have you purchased additional property investments?

03 Has your family grown?

04 Have some of your children left home?

05 Have you changed careers?
( Transitioning from a physically demanding job to something office based may warrant a reassessent to lower premiums, and vice versa).

All of these factors can impact your level of life insurance, trauma insurance, total permanent disability insurance (TPD) and income protection.

### Landlord insurance

If you own rental properties, it's vital to review your landlord insurance at least once a year. Proactively researching and comparing different policies could lead to a more inclusive coverage at a lower cost. As the value of your property portfolio increases, adjust your insurance coverage accordingly to match its value. Keeping your policies up to date aids in risk mitigation and safeguards your investment.

## Car insurance and other risk coverage

Regularly reviewing your car insurance and other types of risk coverage is also prudent practice. Comparing insurance options from different providers can potentially lead to better deals and cost savings. Also check whether you can take advantage of a no claims bonus. And remember – saving money is as good as earning it!

## Mortgage

Taking the time to shop around and compare interest rates can yield significant benefits. And you may not even have to switch banks – simply checking in with your existing bank can often result in rate adjustments. And even a slight difference of 0.5 per cent on a multimillion-dollar property portfolio can result in substantial savings.

Beyond interest rates, it's also worth examining the structure of your mortgage. Consider whether refinancing or adjusting the terms of your loan could be advantageous. This could involve switching from a variable rate to a fixed rate or vice versa, depending on market conditions and your long-term goals.

Don't hesitate to consult with financial professionals or mortgage specialists to explore potential strategies that align with your financial objectives.

## Tax depreciation

At the end of each financial year, property investors can minimise the amount of tax they need to pay through a tax depreciation schedule. This is a report that allows you to claim the natural wear and tear of a property over time.

Tax depreciation schedules can be hugely beneficial for investment property owners, but remain significantly under-utilised. They can not only bring significant tax savings, but also be beneficial should you decide to sell. Providing potential buyers with this information gives them a clear indication of the property's future tax benefits, making it more appealing and potentially raising its market value.

Usually, it pays to seek the assistance of a professional surveyor to conduct these assessments because they have the expertise to identify and quantify all eligible depreciating assets.

### Rent review

If you have your tenants on an annual lease agreement, you should consider whether an adjustment is warranted at the end of each year. If the Consumer Price Index (CPI) has risen significantly, or there has been a change in market conditions, you may want to consider increasing the rent you're charging.

However, when conducting rent reviews, it's important to take into account the quality of your tenants. If they take care of the property and treat it as their own, retaining them may be more beneficial than seeking marginally higher income. Good tenants provide stability, reduce vacancy risks, and protect your investment from potential damage. (Also be aware of any relevant state regulations, which outline how often rent can be increased and how much notice you must give your tenants.)

## QUARTERLY MAINTENANCE

Unfortunately, some money maintenance tasks require attention more than once a year. Here are some of the things you should be monitoring at least every three months.

## Tax and BAS

For those self-employed or managing a business, the quarterly administration of tax and business activity statements (BAS) is imperative. While it can be tempting to prioritise new business opportunities and income generation, overlooking these less-exciting administrative tasks can lead to significant consequences, including heightened audit risks, financial penalties and disruptions to cash flow.

If you have a good accountant, they can help you keep on top of this process, but if you choose to do it yourself, it might be worth formalising a record-keeping system. The Australian Taxation Office offers the following tips:

- Keep records of all sales, fees, expenses, wages and other business costs.

- Keep appropriate records, such as stocktake records and logbooks to substantiate motor vehicle claims.

- Reconcile sales with bank statements.

- Use the correct GST accounting method.

- Keep all your tax invoices and other GST records for five years.

## Superannuation

Every quarter it's worth considering if you can make any extra superannuation contributions, outside of any compulsory payments being made by your employer. At the time of writing, you can make a before-tax contribution of up to $27,500 into your superannuation each year without having to pay extra tax. When possible, it can pay to make that contribution as early in the year as possible to benefit from the effects of compound interest.

Quarterly reviews also provide an opportunity to adjust your superannuation strategy based on changes in your financial situation or goals. Career advancement, salary changes or the addition of new family members may mean you need to consider altering your contributions.

## Investments

While it's true that investments should be evaluated with a long-term perspective, it is still important to identify and address underperformance as quickly as possible. When you notice a particular investment has underachieved over two consecutive quarters, it might be time to consider whether it's worth keeping.

If you have an advisor, talk with them to understand the reasons behind the lacklustre results and explore strategies to rectify the situation. Proactive dialogue fosters transparency and enables timely adjustments, preventing issues from escalating.

## Financial planner meeting

In Australia, financial planners have a legal obligation to revisit client statements and advice annually to ensure the information remains current. However, considering the pace at which markets can change, relying solely on a yearly review is usually not sufficient. Most financial planners recognise this and will suggest a half-yearly review; however, it can pay to be proactive and suggest a quarterly meeting.

## Landlord inspection

If you live in the same city or region as your investment properties, it is highly advisable to check on them once a quarter – whether that's a casual drive-by or a more formal internal inspection. And while it may seem convenient to delegate this responsibility to a letting agent, my experience has shown that their level of care and attention to detail often falls short. Many letting agents will treat your property as just another item on their rent roll, which can result in subpar service and inadequate attention to detail.

I once conducted a personal inspection of an investment property to find the curtains had been burned and there were scorch marks on the bench of a brand-new kitchen. The property manager tried to pass this damage off as 'fair wear and tear', which I disputed. By identifying issues like this early on, you can address them promptly, preventing further damage and potential delays in re-renting the property.

For stand-alone properties, a drive-by inspection can provide valuable insights. The condition of the front yard often reflects how tenants maintain the property as a whole. If you observe neglected surroundings and signs of disarray, it may indicate potential issues inside. Being vigilant in these inspections allows you to address concerns promptly and ensure the overall wellbeing of your investment.

Again, check with the state regulations for where your rental property is located, which outline how often you can conduct formal inspections and how much notice you're required to provide.

## MONTHLY MAINTENANCE

Now that you have a plan for thorough annual and quarterly reviews, it's time to look at the brief but important checks you should carry out on a monthly basis.

### Goals

In chapter 2, we discussed the importance of constantly monitoring your goals to ensure you're moving closer to achieving them. There is no neutral ground in the pursuit of goals – if you haven't made progress, you have inadvertently moved further away. The reality may seem harsh, but it serves as a reminder that time is a finite resource, and every month counts.

Reviewing your goals each month is essential so that you can assess your progress and acknowledge any achievements along the way. Celebrate the milestones you have reached, because they indicate your commitment and dedication.

If your goal is to acquire another property, consider the actions you have taken during the month. Have you actively searched for properties, scoured real estate listings or attended open inspections? By assessing your efforts, you ensure you are actively pursuing your goals rather than passively waiting for opportunities to arise. Remember, hope alone is not a strategy.

If you have a goal to make more money through trading, ask yourself if you've followed your trading plan and monitored your watchlist. Have you consistently engaged with the activities that drive you toward success? These actions demonstrate your commitment to achieving your desired outcomes. Reflect on whether you have actively worked towards your goals during the month.

If you find that you have made little to no progress, it is essential to ask yourself the difficult question: why? While being busy is a common excuse, usually other factors are also at play and it's important to identify them and rectify the situation.

You should also stop to consider whether the goal itself holds true importance to you. If the goal no longer resonates with your aspirations or values, it may be necessary to redefine it and adapt your plan to reflect your evolving perspectives. By regularly reassessing your goals, you can ensure that they remain relevant and align with your evolving vision.

Remember that consistency is key in achieving your goals. Embrace the mantra of 'never break the chain', as advocated by James Clear in his book *Atomic Habits*. Stay committed and motivated, and use each month as an opportunity to inch closer to your desired outcomes.

## Budget

In chapter 3, I outlined how to set a budget and ensure you're sticking to it. Each month, you should look at all of your expenses. Many online budgeting tools can help you with this process – including one available via the online Success Portal that accompanies this book. Using such a tool gives you a comprehensive view of your income, expenses and savings.

Regularly reviewing your budget enables you to assess if you are adhering to it and identify areas that may require adjustments to align with the changing world and your evolving circumstances.

Your budget should be flexible and adaptable to accommodate life's evolving demands. For example, if you have children, their activities and associated expenses may change over time.

Through ongoing budget assessments, you can align your spending with your goals, track your progress, and ensure your financial journey remains on course.

## Powerplay and surge

Once you've assessed your goals, it's time to unleash what I call the powerplay and surge! This is where you choose a single project you want to give unwavering attention to, and then approach with complete determination. This could mean focusing on a particular financial goal, but could also be something related to health and fitness, a relationship or renovation project.

For instance, if your investment property becomes vacant, you might embark on an intensive spruce up to enhance its appeal and increase rental potential. This could involve renovating, painting or improving its overall condition.

A concentrated burst of effort over a long weekend or annual leave can yield remarkable transformations, akin to the awe-inspiring makeovers seen on television shows. By focusing your energy and attention on a specific task, you can significantly add value and expedite progress.

In the realm of investments, a surge may involve delving into research and analysis to identify potential opportunities for growth. The key is to channel your focus and energy into one primary surge each month, allowing you to move the needle significantly. It's like using a magnifying glass to concentrate sunlight on a target, intensifying its impact.

By setting aside time for these surges throughout the year, you create a rhythm of progress and achievement. Each surge propels you closer to your goals, inching you forward with purpose and determination.

## PLAN YOUR ROUTINE!

The table on the following page provides a summary of my recommended annual, quarterly and monthly maintenance.

Now that you're aware of the essential money maintenance tasks, sit down with a planner and mark down when you plan to complete them! Remember, these will be done annually, quarterly or monthly, depending on their nature and significance.

While I don't think it's necessary to conduct reviews on a weekly or daily basis, it can pay to take quick peeks at your account balances to check for any anomalies or pressing issues. If any fraudulent transactions, overdraft fees or declined transactions have occurred, you will want to get onto them quickly.

Your long-term financial success hinges on you remaining in control through a well-honed routine, and if you're a couple, it's important that you are both actively involved. In the next chapter, I introduce the concept of a money 'date night' and explain how it fits into your money maintenance regime!

## Money Maintenance Checklist

| | | |
|---|---|---|
| **Annually** | Full review of all insurance policies | Ask for loyalty discount<br>Check for no claims bonuses |
| | Mortgage | Explore refinance options<br>Look for lower rates |
| | Tax and depreciation reports | Confirm tax deductions on your rental properties |
| | Rent review | Potentially increase rent to boost yield on property |
| **Quarterly** | Tax and BAS | Ensure your tax and especially BAS are up to date |
| | Superannuation | Review the performance of your superannuation, especially versus the market |
| | Investments | Review the performance of your investments, especially versus the broader market |
| | Financial planner meeting | Lock in short quarterly reviews to look at asset allocation, performance and other matters |
| | Landlord inspection | Physically inspect your rental properties with the agent |
| **Monthly** | Goals | Evaluate your progress toward your goals and revise action plans where needed |
| | Budget | Evaluate your budget – are you sticking to it and does it need adjusting? |
| | Powerplay and surge | Significantly increase your focus on any areas that are a new priority |

## 5-POINT ACTION PLAN

1. Establish a system or routine that works for you, and includes annual, quarterly and monthly financial checks. Consistency is key in maintaining financial health.

2. Strive to stay updated about your financial situation. This includes keeping up to date with changes in market conditions, new financial products or regulations that could affect your financial health.

3. Identify and address issues early. Whether it's a slight dip in investment performance, an unexpected expense or an error in your account balance, identifying and addressing issues early can prevent larger financial setbacks down the line.

4. Don't hesitate to seek advice from financial professionals such as accountants, financial advisors and tax specialists. Their expertise can prove invaluable in managing your finances effectively and strategically.

5. Prioritise education. A commitment to learning and being adaptable will ensure that you can adjust your financial strategies to align with your evolving financial goals and the changing market conditions.

## ONLINE RESOURCES

Making sure you keep your plan current and working for you requires maintenance. Access simple to follow and easy to apply checklist and timetables for staying on track at wealthplaybook.com.au.

# Chapter 26

# DATE NIGHT

Money may not buy love, but fighting about it will
bankrupt your relationship.
Michelle Singletary

My wife and I share a bustling home with five children and, amid all the chaos, we manage to carve out time each week for a dedicated date night. This ritual has become an integral part of our marriage.

Typically, these weekly catch-ups are spent discussing the day-to-day happenings in our lives and the lives of our children. However, once every month, these casual chats make way for a more focused 'money date', which involves taking a deep dive into our finances. We meticulously review our budget, monitor our savings and investments, strategise for imminent expenses and realign our financial goals if necessary.

While this might sound unromantic and somewhat obsessive, we've discovered that these money dates maintain not only our financial success but also the vitality of our relationship.

Financial disagreements are among the leading causes of divorce worldwide, so continuing to have an open dialogue on such matters is important! Transparency is fundamental in a relationship and regular discussions about money can prevent misunderstandings and foster mutual trust.

I should note that even if you're single, taking the time to schedule a monthly evening to delve into your finances is still highly beneficial. As a bachelor, I would regularly reserve a table at my local restaurant and meticulously jot down budgeting and investing notes on a paper table cloth, which I would then take home and implement. That might seem a bit sad and lonely, but it helped me get to where I am today!

## THE IMPORTANCE OF ROUTINE

Too many people choose to re-evaluate their financial position only once a year, either as a New Year's resolution or as part of an end of financial year review. Unfortunately, such infrequent assessments can lead to missed opportunities or problems being identified too late.

These days, the economy and markets can turn very quickly, making it essential to stay on top of your financial situation and be ready to adapt. I recommend making your money date a fixed, monthly appointment in your calendar. Choose a date that works for you and stick to it every month.

You may also choose to occasionally involve your accountant or advisor in these money dates, or perhaps schedule separate regular meetings with them.

## THE PERFECT MONEY DATE

A money date isn't just about numbers and spreadsheets. It's an opportunity to come together in a relaxed environment, away from the usual distractions of home, to have open and honest discussions about financial goals and strategies.

## CASE STUDY: TRADING TEAM

One of my clients and his wife have built a substantial nest egg by working together to manage their self-managed superannuation fund.

In the partnership, my client, an experienced trader and investor, is responsible for market analysis and key decision-making, but it's his wife who executes and manages all of the trades.

This assignment of roles is strategic. If something unexpected were to happen to my client, his wife wouldn't be left in the dark. She would have the knowledge and understanding to continue managing their investments.

Further to that, the arrangement provides a psychological advantage by drawing a clear line between the decision-making and execution process and ensuring trades are made objectively.

The couple has also found that working together creates a sense of mutual trust and accountability.

Here are some essential tips to help you plan your perfect money date:

- *Escape the four walls:* Stepping out of your home for a date can provide a distraction-free environment, vital for focused financial discussions. While it might require hiring a babysitter, the pay-off in the form of undisturbed, productive conversation is well worth it.

- *Set the tone:* Remember, this is a date, not a business meeting. Strive for a relaxed atmosphere, perhaps incorporating a favourite meal. Keep the conversation positive and solution-oriented.

- *Plan the conversation:* Create an agenda for your discussion, whether it involves a budget review, financial goal setting or investment strategy. This planning can keep the conversation focused and fruitful.

- *Encourage open dialogue and active listening:* Facilitate space for both partners to voice their concerns, ideas and expectations. Mutual understanding fosters financial empathy and cooperation.

- *Celebrate the victories:* Use your money date nights to commemorate financial achievements, regardless of their magnitude. Celebrating these milestones can reinforce positive financial habits and drive you towards larger goals. If you've had a good month, feel free to pop a bottle of champagne!

## START THE HABIT

A money date night might seem unconventional, but trust me, the rewards will be significant! It's not just about dollars and cents, but ensuring that if you're in a relationship, you are growing stronger as a couple.

If you intend to spend a lifetime with someone, it's essential to invest time in nurturing that relationship.

## 5-POINT ACTION PLAN

1. Make it a habit to set aside a fixed, monthly appointment in your calendar for a dedicated money date night. If you have a partner, choose a date that works for both of you and commit to sticking to it consistently.

2. Step out of your home for your money date nights to create a distraction-free environment. Consider going to a favourite restaurant, taking a walk in the park, or finding a cosy spot where you can have uninterrupted conversations.

3. Plan your money date discussions by creating an agenda. Identify the key financial topics you both want to cover, such as budget review, savings and investments, financial goals and any upcoming expenses.

4. During your money date nights, provide space for both you and your partner to express your concerns, ideas and expectations regarding your finances. Encourage open dialogue and active listening, allowing each other to contribute to the conversation.

5. Use your money date nights as an opportunity to celebrate your financial achievements, regardless of their size. Whether you've reached a savings goal, paid off a debt or made a successful investment, take the time to acknowledge and commemorate these victories.

## ONLINE RESOURCES

Check out the online Success Portal at wealthplaybook.com for more on date night.

# Part V

# YOUR PLAYBOOK

# Chapter 27

# THE SIX PHASES
# OF YOUR PLAYBOOK

Life is not a spectator sport; it only rewards action takers.

Andrew Baxter

Congratulations on reaching the end of the book! This final chapter is where I provide a playbook for applying everything you've learned. It's a practical roadmap that will help you navigate each phase of your life to ensure you're enjoying the 'now' while also preparing for the 'later'!

For the purposes of the guide, I have divided your investing life into six phases:

1. Starting out (age 10–20)
2. Aggressive investing (age 20–30)
3. Accumulation (age 30–40)
4. Wealth explosion (age 40–50)
5. Pre-retirement (age 50–60)
6. Retirement (age 60+)

Now, if you already find yourself in one of the later phases, don't stress. Remember, it's never too late to start planning for your financial future and making informed decisions that can improve your circumstances.

My advice would be to look at the earlier life phases and determine what groundwork you need to catch up on. It may be that you need to work a little harder to save a little more than someone in your age group who started earlier.

Regardless, please make sure you are tackling each phase in sequential order. This will ensure you see a steady rise and controlled decline of your net worth, as shown in the following figure.

**The Six Life Phases**

| Age 10-20 'Starting out' | Age 20-30 'Agressive investing' | Age 30-40 'Accumulation' | Age 40-50 'Wealth explosion' | Age 50-60 'Pre-retirement' | Age 60+ 'Retirement' |

# PHASE 1: STARTING OUT
## (Ideal age 10–20)

| | |
|---|---|
| **Phase description** | This phase is all about learning and understanding the basics of personal finance and money management. If you're lucky, your parents or educators may be teaching you some of these concepts; if not, take the initiative and educate yourself. |
| | Remember the importance of learning how to be disciplined enough to follow a strict budget and save money. |
| | During this time, you should also start thinking about exactly what it is you want out of life. |
| **Key objectives** | • Gain employment, or a part-time job if you're studying<br>• Save for an emergency fund and a house deposit<br>• Make a head start on retirement contributions<br>• Set goals for the future and what you want to achieve in life |
| **Risk profile** | Aggressive |
| **Appropriate asset classes** | • High-interest savings accounts<br>• Growth stocks<br>• ETFs |
| **Helpful chapters from this book** | • Chapter 2: Goal setting<br>• Chapter 3: Budgeting basics<br>• Chapter 7: Pocket money<br>• Chapter 14: Direct share investments<br>• Chapter 15: Exchange-traded funds |

# PHASE 2: AGGRESSIVE INVESTING
## (Ideal age 20–30)

| | |
|---|---|
| **Phase description** | This is a very important period where you are kickstarting your career and focusing on higher earnings. However, it's important that as your income starts to increase, your lifestyle expenses remain as low as possible.<br><br>Any surplus cash flow should be funnelled into higher risk, higher growth investments. You're young and have time on your side to recover from potential financial losses.<br><br>It may also be a time to educate yourself on trading and other forms of investing, while beginning to think about your best investing structure and how to maximise your tax benefits. |
| **Key objectives** | • Pay off student debt<br>• Kickstart your career<br>• Increase income<br>• Increase emergency savings<br>• Purchase your own home by age 25<br>• Purchase your first investment property by age 28<br>• Begin saving for children's education |
| **Risk profile** | Aggressive |
| **Appropriate asset classes** | • Property<br>• High-growth stocks<br>• ETFs |
| **Helpful chapters from this book** | • Chapter 8: Start with a safety net<br>• Chapter 11: Investing in education<br>• Chapter 18: Your home<br>• Chapter 19: Investment properties |

# PHASE 3: ACCUMULATION
## (Ideal age 30–40)

| | |
|---|---|
| **Phase description** | The accumulation phase represents a critical time for wealth building. <br><br> By the time you're in your thirties, you're likely to have a more substantial income than you did in your twenties, offering a unique opportunity to accelerate your wealth accumulation efforts. <br><br> With increased financial stability, you can aggressively grow your investment portfolio. This could involve investing in diverse assets such as stocks, bonds and real estate, or even starting a side hustle. <br><br> During this phase, you should prioritise the repayment of high-interest debts to reduce your financial burden, enabling you to redirect more resources towards wealth creation. This can set the stage for robust financial health in your later years. |
| **Key objectives** | • Consider transitioning to a self-managed super fund (SMSF) with your partner <br> • Factor in new expenses if starting a family <br> • Consider purchasing more investment properties as rental income begins to accumulate <br> • Further develop your wealth growth strategy <br> • Begin planning for retirement |
| **Risk profile** | Moderate to aggressive |
| **Appropriate asset classes** | • Property <br> • Stocks <br> • ETFs |
| **Helpful chapters from this book** | • Chapter 5: The side hustle <br> • Chapter 21: Your investing structure <br> • Chapter 22: Superannuation |

# PHASE 4: WEALTH EXPLOSION
## (Ideal age 40–50)

| | |
|---|---|
| **Phase description** | The wealth explosion phase, typically occurring between ages 40 and 50, represents a significant turning point in an individual's financial journey. During this decade, the power of compounding truly starts to kick in, leading to a significant increase in wealth. This phase also provides an opportunity to diversify investments further, manage risk effectively and focus on tax-efficient strategies, ultimately solidifying your financial stability for the forthcoming retirement years. |
| **Key objectives** | • Review and rebalance your portfolio<br>• Ensure you have maximum income insurance<br>• Consider changes to your investment structure to ensure you are receiving maximum tax benefits<br>• Consider allocating a small percentage of your portfolio to high-growth 'exotic' investments |
| **Risk profile** | Moderate |
| **Appropriate asset classes** | • Property<br>• Stocks<br>• ETFs<br>• Exotics |
| **Helpful chapters from this book** | • Chapter 16: Exotics<br>• Chapter 23: Insurance<br>• Chapter 25: Money maintenance |

# PHASE 5: PRE-RETIREMENT
## (Ideal age 50–60)

| | |
|---|---|
| **Phase description** | The pre-retirement phase signifies an important transition period. The focus shifts to retiring debt, a step that's crucial in ensuring a comfortable, stress-free retirement. For instance, a 55 year old with six or seven investment properties might consider selling half of them.<br><br>Negative gearing, commonly used in the accumulation phase, should be replaced by a positive income flow, derived from owning clear-title income-generating properties. This careful debt management strategy ensures a secure and stable income stream for the upcoming retirement years. |
| **Key objectives** | • Retire debt<br>• Consider selling some investment properties<br>• De-risk investments |
| **Risk profile** | Moderate to Conservative |
| **Appropriate asset classes** | • Dividend-paying stocks<br>• Property<br>• ETFs |
| **Helpful chapters from this book** | • Chapter 20: Dynamics of planning<br>• Chapter 24: Times of crisis |

# PHASE 6: RETIREMENT
## (Ideal age 60+)

| | |
|---|---|
| **Phase description** | This is the time to enjoy the fruits of your labour. However, managing your money in retirement is just as important as building it. You'll now have a fixed income so you'll need to watch what you spend! |
| **Key objectives** | • Return to budgeting<br>• Reduce life insurance and income protection<br>• Review your estate plans regularly, ensuring your will, trusts and beneficiary designations are up to date<br>• Protect your capital by ensuring you have a diverse portfolio |
| **Risk profile** | Conservative |
| **Appropriate asset classes** | • Dividend-paying stocks<br>• Property<br>• ETFs |
| **Helpful chapters from this book** | • Chapter 20: Dynamics of planning<br>• Chapter 23: Insurance<br>• Chapter 25: Money maintenance |

# CONCLUSION

Firstly, massive congratulations on finishing this book – I trust you enjoyed it! My hope is that *The Wealth Playbook* has given you a solid game plan for building your wealth and living your best life.

My goal in writing this book was very simple: to help everyday Australians safely navigate the world of investing and be able to enjoy a life that is free of money worries, financial uncertainty and feeling overwhelmed, through a series of simple, practical steps.

Leaving a legacy is a powerful driver and, in just the same way that I trust this book helps you create a better future for you and yours, the lens I have used for the book structure is both practical and based on the advice I am giving my own children, as they embark on their journey into the world of investing.

By taking a more active interest in your own personal wealth journey, from this day forward, you are far more likely to enjoy financial success and, perhaps most importantly, avoid being exploited by the investing universe and players within it.

While you may have reached the end of this book, this is just the beginning of the next chapter in your financial success. To help you continue to grow your knowledge skills and confidence, alongside the book, I have developed an online Success Portal that is jam-packed with useful tools, free education, training and further resources to help you implement any area of your wealth journey, and I highly encourage you to check these out. The link to access all of this is wealthplaybook.com.au.

Success in the world of investing, rather like anywhere in life, rarely comes by accident. It requires focused effort, clarity of planning and choosing the correct vehicle to get there. The Success Portal is designed to provide you with these tools and more, so please feel free to take what you want from there.

When I look at my life, and the lessons learned, probably like you, I think to myself, *If only I'd* . . . For most people the rest of that thought is one of two things:

*If only I'd started sooner* . . .

Or

*If only I'd known that before I started* . . .

By following the pathway laid out in this book and the accompanying Success Portal, you should be able to enjoy greater financial success, more quickly, with less confusion, and avoid many of the pitfalls that can derail your progress.

The time to start on that journey is right now and with the plan laid out in this book as your roadmap!

It is humbling to be your coach, guide and mentor, and I hope that the tools and the strategies provided help you successfully start your journey to create tomorrow's wealth today.